Holistic Shakespe

Holistic Shakespeare
An Experiential Learning Approach

Debra Charlton

intellect Bristol, UK / Chicago, USA

First published in the UK in 2012 by
Intellect, The Mill, Parnall Road, Fishponds, Bristol, BS16 3JG, UK

First published in the USA in 2012 by
Intellect, The University of Chicago Press, 1427 E. 60th Street,
Chicago, IL 60637, USA

A catalogue record for this book is available from the
British Library.

Cover designer: Persephone Coelho
Copy-editor: MPS Technologies
Production manager: Jessica Mitchell
Typesetting: Planman Technologies

ISBN 978-1-84150-471-1

Printed and bound by Hobbs, UK

Contents

Preface

In his book, *Shakespeare's Advice to the Players*, acclaimed director Peter Hall predicts that within 200 years, Shakespeare "will only be faintly visible—rather as Chaucer is to us. ... He will soon need translating" (2003, p. 10). Distanced by centuries of cultural, linguistic, and educational change, modern teachers of Shakespeare face formidable challenges as they strive to help their students discover meaningful connections between 400 year-old canonical plays and the pressing concerns of an increasingly complex twenty-first century world. Conventional desk-bound instructional methods, centered primarily in left-brain thinking, can heighten these barriers and stifle appreciation of the plays' vigor, beauty, and sustained relevance.

This book is designed to overcome these obstacles by drawing on the methodologies and values of the holistic educational model, which is directed toward whole-brain, integrated, and experiential learning that motivates students to think deeply about the interlinks between what they learn in the classroom and the significant moral and ethical questions that impact their everyday lives. The content and exercises in this book, which are equally applicable and pertinent to either literary or theatre classroom settings, combine analytical and intuitive learning approaches to foster personalized growth of the whole student. Regardless of where each student's educational comfort zone might lie, he/she is encouraged to immerse fully in both performative and academic activities, shedding inhibiting self-labels along the way.

Many colleagues have lent their professional and personal encouragement during the writing of this book. My gratitude goes to Dr. John Fleming, Chair of the Department of Theatre and Dance at Texas State University-San Marcos, for his generosity and unfaltering guidance, and to my colleague, Dr. Charles Ney, a fellow Shakespeare enthusiast who has been an encouraging and insightful faculty mentor throughout this process. I also extend deep thanks to Patricia Delorey of the Asolo Conservatory for Actor Training, my teaching partner in the Texas at Stratford Shakespeare intensive, and to our gracious host-facilitators for the program, Dr. Paul Edmondson and the staff of the Shakespeare Birthplace Trust at Stratford-upon-Avon. Through their passion and curiosity, my students push me to constantly reassess my own ingrained assumptions about classroom Shakespeare, and I relish all that they continue to teach me. Finally, I dedicate this book to my daughters, Ashley and Olivia, for their patience and support.

Introduction

S hakespeare and his contemporaries perceived man's mind, body, spirit, and environment as inextricably interconnected. This holistic mindset, the foundation of scientific and medical thought during the Renaissance era, profoundly influenced art and literature throughout the period and supplied the ideological cornerstone of Shakespeare's dramaturgy. In the modern classroom, recapturing this lost holistic viewpoint offers an invaluable resource for encountering Shakespeare's plays with greater depth, clarity, and authenticity.

Three intertwined concepts made up the fabric of holistic thought during Shakespeare's lifetime: Wholeness, Interconnectivity, and Embodiment. Borrowed, adapted, and refined from classical and medieval philosophies, this triad of holistic values comprised one of the most significant theoretical influences on Shakespeare's stagecraft. Collectively, these core tenets, which Shakespeare absorbed from earliest childhood, indelibly colored his perspective on the world in which he lived, while providing the wellspring for his creation of character and situation, and sustaining the ethical systems that underpin the fictional world of the plays. These seminal values, which are discussed in greater depth in Chapter 1, also support the framework for the holistic curricular approach outlined in the ensuing chapters. In the holistic Shakespeare classroom, application of these foundational concepts opens up a fertile pathway that leads students toward a more intimate understanding of how Shakespeare thought—about himself, his relationships, and his environment.

In holistic education, WHOLENESS (or holism) describes an integrated curricular approach that places value on the complete learner and cultivates every student's unique potential to become active, thinking, and caring contributors to the larger world. In contrast to conventional curricular approaches, which locate primary focus on the learner's acquisition of formulaic essential knowledge and skills, the holistic educational approach draws upon the rich resources of intuition, memory, sensation, and imagination as channels for personalized discovery. Of course, time-honored analytical and critical tools are not discarded; instead, within a supportive and exploratory classroom community, students are encouraged to engage in the constant interplay between cognitive polarities. Like Shakespeare's dramatic language, which fluctuates between restrained, highly patterned rhetorical structures and unpredictable, impassioned syncopation, the holistic Shakespeare classroom stresses the plurality of teaching strategies necessary to convey content and facilitate communication of the expressive meaning of Shakespeare's multilayered plays; instructional techniques that target students' analytical reasoning skills are deliberately juxtaposed against those that favor subjective, individualized responses, and experiential activities that motivate freeform creative play are balanced by those that foster introspective contemplation. Students learn to practice wholeness through both inner reflection and collaborative activities that enhance personal and transpersonal awareness. By accentuating the unity of the complete learning organism, the holistic model invites students to become adaptable, fluid, and self-aware learners, who are open to experimentation and not intimidated by the unfamiliar.

Holistic education is, by nature, value-based and student-centered. It is concerned with nurturing the whole learner, not just when he/she occupies a seat in the classroom but also when he/she ventures beyond the classroom doorway. Naturally, all skilled and compassionate instructors recognize that learners lead complicated lives both inside and outside the school walls; in their daily lives, every student grapples with significant, often daunting, ethical challenges. However, traditional educational models, which concentrate almost exclusively on the intellectual life of students, provide inadequate footholds to bridge the gap between classroom and real life growth opportunities.

Holistic learning promotes students' moral intelligence, without privileging any single value system. It fosters growth of the WHOLE learner—intellectual, aesthetic, and spiritual—by:

- Training students to think deeply about the world they inhabit and to develop heightened sensitivity to humanitarian values.

- Honing the aesthetic, spiritual, and intellectual skills students need to become active and compassionate global citizens.

- Motivating learners to translate classroom discoveries into real-world situations and actions that will bring positive change to society.

- Inviting students to unpeel layers of meaning and pose questions about the "why" of learning: Why is this content significant to my life? What can it teach me about the ways in which I engage with others? How does this knowledge contribute to my understanding of the natural world and the greater human community?

Early in their public schooling, most students are quickly immersed in atomistic, rather than holistic, educational settings (Pask and Scott 1972; Svensson 1984). Atomistic (or mechanistic) curricular approaches tend to break content down into small parts made up of isolated facts and details. Learning objectives are often heavily slanted toward boosting scores on standardized tests, while contextualization is virtually ignored. Atomistic teaching shifts emphasis away from the needs of the individual learner in favor of regimented instruction geared toward the memorization (but not retention, application, or true understanding) of limited, particular content.

In America, an upsurge in emphasis on atomistic teaching was one inevitable byproduct of educational "reforms" of the 1980s and 1990s. During those decades, student outcomes became increasingly tied to government funding, with scores on achievement tests becoming artificial, but hotly pursued, indicators of student, teacher, and institutional success. Today, "teaching to the test" has become the residual fallout of this fixation on test scores, which has led to oversimplification of content by instructors, excessive use of short-term learning devices, such as rote drills, and the engenderment of a competitive learning environment directed toward individual student achievement at the sacrifice of classroom collegiality. Opponents of both atomistic teaching and standardized testing have long criticized the underlying assumption that there exists a predetermined set of "universal knowledge" that should be mastered by every student, and point out the resultant neglect of this educational philosophy to promote positive but nontestable human attributes, such as emotional accessibility, compassion, nurturance, and imagination (Kohn 2000).

In contrast to the atomistic educational approach typical of most modern teaching systems, the holistic classroom is devoted to systemic learning in which each curricular part is viewed within the context of the larger whole. New content is tied to both previous knowledge and individual life experience. Since no topic is taught in a contextual vacuum, students are challenged to do more than merely memorize random facts or master disconnected skills. Instead, focus is placed on INTERCONNECTIVITY between discrete areas of learning. Like theatre-making itself, holistic classroom Shakespeare celebrates the convergence of individual talents. Team-building, often modeled by team-teaching, transforms the Shakespeare classroom into a true scholarly and creative community, where students debate divergent readings, brainstorm about how to stage a scene, or share personal sensory responses or emotional recollections evoked by the plays. In the holistic classroom, Shakespeare's plays are simultaneously experienced as historical artifacts, works of poetry, philosophical texts, and above all, as living theatrical vehicles. This unified learning experience echoes the rich intellectual and creative climate that molded Shakespeare into a consummate holistic thinker.

In the holistic Shakespeare classroom, teacher-driven learning material is partnered by student-centered experiential activities. Students practice EMBODIMENT of Shakespeare's words, ideas, and characters through full engagement of the body/voice. They stage scenes, exploring space and composition, examining character motivations and locating the human conflict at the core of every dramatic situation. They register Shakespeare's language through its taste and feel in the "gymnasium of the mouth," to borrow renowned voice teacher Kristen Linklater's evocative phrase (1992, p. 20), and illustrate character alliances and social hierarchies through physicalization exercises. Holistic Shakespeare embraces the text's definitive status as a theatrical script, making performance-based activities an indispensable instructional tool. Like the exciting creative buzz that pervades the rehearsal room, the holistic learning environment is active, process-oriented, cooperative, and exploratory, which restores true ownership of the educational journey to the place where it belongs—in the hands of the student.

Performance-based teaching has reinvigorated the Shakespeare classroom in recent decades. Numerous books on the topic have helped nontheatre teachers gain confidence integrating drama-based activities, such as breathing exercises, scene work, and relaxation techniques, into their pedagogical repertoire (Gibson 1998; Riggio 1999; and

Rocklin 2005). This volume seeks to enrich that melding of teaching strategies, while promoting the following unique goals of holistic education: liminality; synergy; and empowerment.

Liminality

The holistic Shakespeare classroom represents a liminal space, an open threshold between left- and right-brain learning that encourages free navigation between expressive and analytical modes of thought. As actor/scholars working within this liminal space, students are encouraged to explore their latent talents, to stretch and experiment in a lively, emotionally safe, and dynamic learning environment. They will learn to cultivate a state of creative receptivity that allows for spontaneity, empathy, growth, and change. The poet Keats described this willingness to experience "uncertainties, mysteries, and doubts" as "negative capability," a quality which Shakespeare possessed in abundance (quoted in Hirst 1981). This "in-between" state of being is not confined by rigid compartmentalization or limiting self-definitions. Instead, conventional instructional boundaries are removed to facilitate an organic learning process rooted in the exploration of collaborative partnerships, intellectual freedom, and self-expression.

Synergy

Theatre, the most collaborative of art forms, is the product of a unique artistic synergy built on the diverse talents of the production ensemble. The holistic Shakespeare classroom draws inspiration from this synergistic model. Conventional instructor-driven teaching methodologies give place to facilitation, guidance, and mediation, permitting every participant to become both a teacher and a learner. High value is centered on consensual decision-making, negotiation and cooperation, through which students discover that collective creation is greater than the sum of its parts.

Empowerment

Holistic education stresses the intersection between learning and personal and community empowerment. Knowledge brings not only individual growth and moral development but also the responsibility to use our heightened social sensibility for the common good. Shakespeare's plays pose probing moral questions that transcend the walls of the classroom or theatre. By sharing Shakespeare's insights into the human condition, students can grow to become thoughtful and active citizens who are motivated to leave a positive imprint on the world we share.

In Chapter 1, we consider a provocative question: "How did Shakespeare think?" As this chapter explains, Shakespeare's remarkable intellectual and artistic duality was not merely the result of fortuitous DNA. A holistic perspective conditioned through cultural and educational osmosis stimulated his unique genius. This chapter examines early modern beliefs about the mind/body/spirit connection and explores a recurrent motif in Shakespeare's plays, the continuity between individual human action and civic and cosmic harmony. We will also look at the school system that educated Shakespeare and its influence on his growth as a thinker and writer.

Chapter 1 lays out the conceptual framework for the practical learning process outlined in the next four chapters, which study four Shakespearean plays through the lens of holistic thought: *A Midsummer Night's Dream, Measure for Measure, Othello,* and *The Tempest*. Each chapter is intended to serve as a supportive companion on the intellectual, emotional, and spiritual journey of bringing Shakespeare's plays to life in the classroom. Built around a significant social or environmental topic addressed in the focal play, every chapter is organized into five learning modules, which may be taught individually or as a complete instructional unit. A contextual essay, intended to provide the instructor with the background information necessary to guide class conversations and activities, introduces each unit. Each chapter contains a set of diverse practical activities directed toward developing creative accessibility, analytical skills, community awareness, and emotional responsiveness, thereby comprising a practical teaching manual for a specific play text.

Chapter 2 investigates *A Midsummer Night's Dream* from an eco-conscious perspective. It explores the relationship between the characters and their natural world, focusing on the mystique of the lost wilderness, which Shakespeare posits as a restorative retreat for self-discovery and personal healing. During Shakespeare's lifetime, many of the wilderness spaces of the English countryside were forever lost due to privatization and development; therefore, we look at two contemporary environmental topics, the enclosure movement that generated controversy around the time of the play's composition and the massive deforestation that had decimated the ecological heritage of Shakespeare's native Warwickshire only a few generations before. We examine these topics' possible influence on the play's setting, and consider contrasting directorial and design interpretations of the play's green spaces. Finally, a set of theatre-based exercises is designed to heighten sensitivity to the relationship between self and space.

In Chapter 3 the ethical use of personal and public power provides the framework for the study of *Measure for Measure*. In this puzzling work, Shakespeare raises probing moral questions, but fails to provide definitive answers. The play's ethical ambiguity lends the text surprising modernity. Written during an age of extraordinary promise and transition, the play reflects the Tudor era's newfound opportunities for personal advancement through individual initiative and education, rather than the mere accident of birth, following centuries of relative social fixity. However, just as it does today, greater individual power brought increased temptation for exploitation of those less fortunate. *In Measure for Measure*, Shakespeare dramatizes complex power issues, like body ownership and government intervention in private affairs that remain just as pertinent today as when the play was written. The activities contained in this section introduce students to theatre-centered explorations of power, justice, and status based on the active learning techniques of Augusto Boal and the Theatre of the Oppressed.

Othello provides a vehicle for studying the rhetoric of hate in Chapter 4. The plot's central conflict and tragic, violent conclusion are precipitated by Iago's insidious use of hate language to manipulate, isolate, and divide the other characters. In Shakespeare's England, racial prejudice was an accepted part of the social hierarchy. Sadly, although almost 400 years have passed since the play was written, the language of hate continues to be a destructive force in modern society. This chapter delves into Shakespeare's use of hate propaganda as a powerful dramatic device. It also examines Elizabethan ideas about race and gender and considers how Shakespeare subverts social norms by depicting a mixed race marriage based on love and equality. Historical casting practices are considered to reflect changing directorial attitudes toward the play's racial theme. Practical activities in this chapter explore themes of hate, prejudice, and social division through the radically contrasting methodologies of two revolutionary theatre artists, Antonin Artaud and Bertolt Brecht.

Holistic education turns to both scientific and spiritual traditions to teach respect for inner life and the mystery of existence. The interactions and tensions between science and spirituality ground the discussion of *The Tempest* in Chapter 5. Perhaps no Shakespearean play better exemplifies the author's fascination with metaphysics than this enigmatic romance set on a deserted tropical island. In his play, Shakespeare relies on music and magic to weave a fantasy tale about splintered family relationships. Written during a period of avid popular interest in scientific discoveries and New World expeditions, the play is concerned with possibilities that transcend rational explanation and the realm of the known. Built around a relatively static plot, it is Shakespeare's most abstract and philosophical work, probing the line between illusion and reality, physical science and the supernatural. This chapter studies the play's treatment of magic, alchemy, astronomy, and the occult, while also examining its influence on modern science fiction and the relatively new "science play" genre. The intersection between analytical fields of study, spirituality, and art forms the basis of the practical exercises in this section.

A final section contains resources for further study. Materials include a glossary of terms, suggestions for further reading, and pointers to teaching aids, including web materials, films, music, and visual art that further illuminate the focal plays.

The Shakespeare canon represents a theatrical microcosm of the most pressing ethical questions that still consume humanity almost four centuries after the dramatist's death. Through constructive dialogue and deep engagement with the complex issues examined in Shakespeare's plays—class difference, racial tensions, violence, gender stereotyping, self-identity, destruction of our natural resources—students learn to read the plays actively, intuitively, and empathically. While many Shakespeare teachers note the superficiality of their students' reading of the plays, the holistic learner connects with the script on a mature, multidimensional level. The constraints of conformity and uniformity, and the search for a single "right" answer yield place to respect for difference and mutual tolerance. As students discover meaningful correlations between curricular content and their own life challenges, learning becomes a highly personal journey that nourishes genuine self-knowledge.

In *The Republic*, Plato asserts that "compulsory learning never sticks in the mind" (Lee 2003, p. 269). Holistic teaching helps students rediscover the wonder of learning by emphasizing self-motivation and choice. Shakespeare's plays offer a rich medium for encouraging holistic thought. His dramatic works straddle artificial boundaries between academic and creative curricula, serving as ideal conduits for the holistic educational model, which seeks to teach the complete student through a systemic, experiential curriculum that engages the whole mind, body, and spirit. Holistic education promotes healthy interpersonal relationships, ethical values, and concern for the global community. It also develops heightened awareness of our ecological responsibilities and encourages students to find personal meaning in academic content. Through application of the holistic model to Shakespeare studies, we can help our students discover the plays' continuing relevance to their personal lives and their roles within the larger human family.

Chapter 1

Thinking Like Shakespeare

What a piece of work is a man, how noble in reason, how infinite in faculties, in form
and moving, how express and admirable, in action, how like an angel, in apprehension,
how like a god! the beauty of the world; the paragon of animals. . . .
(Hamlet, II, ii, 303–7)

Shakespeare was a quintessential holistic thinker. Nature had gifted him with an
extraordinary aptitude to navigate fluidly between the realms of intellect and
imagination. Through his dramatic writing, Shakespeare found the ideal vehicle for the
exploration and refinement of his abundant talents. Even the playwright's contemporaries
marveled at his twin facility for deep intellectual engagement and creative expressiveness.
In the memorial First Folio, fellow actor Richard Condell wrote, "[Shakespeare's] hand and
mind went together, and what he thought, he uttered with that easiness that we have scarce
received from him a blot in his papers." Of course, such effort comes harder for ordinary
mortals. In the modern Shakespeare classroom, encouraging modes of thought more closely
aligned with the playwright's holistic mindset can optimize students' mental flexibility,
comprehension, and receptivity. By learning to think like Shakespeare, we can acquire a
deeper appreciation and enjoyment of his plays.

Poised on the Corpus Callosum

Both Shakespeare's cultural environment and his natural gifts contributed to his exceptional
intellectual flexibility. Borrowing from the parlance of modern neuroscience, Shakespeare
might be described as "intellectually ambidextrous." Mental-sidedness or dexterity refers
to a person's natural inclination toward either right- or left-brain thinking. Of course,
everyone is born with the potential to utilize both right- and left-brain functions. Everyday
life demands constant transition and communication between cerebral regions in order to
accomplish the myriad tasks that require our attention. Just as a dance teacher or an athletic
coach can train students to fully utilize both sides of the body despite dominant physical
sidedness, an intellectually open classroom setting can also cultivate mental ambidexterity
in students. The holistic Shakespeare classroom both requires and encourages this open and
intellectually flexible learner.

As children, uninhibited imaginative play, centered predominantly in right-brain
modalities, is encouraged and rewarded. But when youngsters enter school, they quickly

discover that most conventional instruction favors left-brain learners. Consequently, early learners make unconscious efforts to harness their uniqueness and individuality to fit within the narrow confines of the traditional classroom. Self-labeling and conformity are the inevitable results, producing vestigial learners who are inhibited from accessing their full intellectual capacity (Rubenzer 1982). Holistic teaching seeks to reunify this vestigial learner.

Brain functions are divided into two distinct but complementary hemispheres, each governing specific skills and ways of processing information (see Molfese and Segalowitz, 1988). Organically, the left side of the brain controls linear, analytical thinking, stores and processes facts and details, and develops problem-solving strategies. The left-brain also facilitates categorization and labeling and allows for comprehension of the past and present. Classroom activities that rely on left-brain functions promote precision, logic, and orderliness. In Shakespeare studies, students might engage this area of the brain through scansion and scoring exercises that foster recognition of language patterns, parts, and groupings, or by compiling data that compares everyday living conditions in Elizabethan England with those of the modern era. Most mathematicians and scientists incline naturally toward left-brain thinking. In contrast, many people with artistic temperaments gravitate toward right-brain activities and thought patterns. Right-brain-sidedness governs abstract thought, artistic ability, and spatial awareness. It allows appreciation of the whole, grasps interdependences between parts of instructional material, facilitates conceptual and abstract thinking, expresses states of being, and is future oriented. Right-brain learners tend to favor subjective and imaginative classroom activities and demonstrate a natural proclivity for interpretive exercises and theoretical content. Teachers of Shakespeare might develop right-brain learning by eliciting students' personal readings of symbolism or imagery, or encourage proclivity for spatial awareness through hands-on exercises like set design, movement activities, or stage blocking. Visualization, music, dance, and other sensory-based media, rather than language, are powerful resources for tapping into the right-brained student's potential for nonverbal learning.

The topic of brain hemispheric functions has sparked a wealth of provocative literature in the past decade, including Daniel Pink's phenomenal bestseller, *A Whole New Brain: Moving from the Information Age to the Conceptual Age* (2005). Recent science has made significant advances in deciphering the correlation between language cognition and brain regions, and proven that brain hemispheric lateralization is not as fixed and compartmentalized as previously believed (see Sahin, Pinker, Cash, Schomer, and Halgren 2009). The human brain has been likened to a parallel processor because of its ability to simultaneously receive and process stimuli in opposing cerebral regions. Language studies have revealed, for example, that expressive vocalization, which includes inflection, intonation, pitch, stress, and rhythm (essential tools for effective communication and performance) is usually lateralized in the right brain, while literal language functions like grammar and vocabulary most often originate in the left brain (see Pinker 1994; Deacon 1997; Brown and Hagoort 2001). Some language functions, however, appear to be controlled bilaterally. Thus coherent and expressive verbal communication, like most other human activities, requires free access to both sides of the brain. Anatomically, the corpus callosum, a band of connective neural fibers, links left- and right-brain hemispheres. In the holistic Shakespeare classroom, students are encouraged to envision themselves as poised on that vital cerebral bridge, ready to travel along this open pathway between discrete ways of learning.

The Holistic Triad: Wholeness, Interconnectivity, and Embodiment

As discussed in the Introduction, holistic classroom Shakespeare embraces three core values: wholeness, interconnectivity, and embodiment. A cultural environment that placed value on systemic thought and cultivation of the WHOLE individual enhanced Shakespeare's natural proclivity for holistic thought. Contrary to popular misconceptions, holistic ideology is not a New Age phenomenon; its roots stretch back to the classical era when great thinkers including Aristotle, Plato, and the physician-philosopher Galen contemplated the relationship between man and his environment, and developed an integrated, systemic worldview rooted in appreciation for the whole of human potential. In the Renaissance era, a resurgence of interest in the writings of the Greek and Roman philosophers reawakened the holistic viewpoint, which in turn became a key influence on humanist learning. By Shakespeare's lifetime, holistic thought imbued every aspect of Elizabethan/Jacobean culture, from humanist education to philosophy to the sciences, providing one of the most profound influences on Shakespeare's perceptions of the world in which he lived.

The golden age of Tudor civilization honored the polymath as the pinnacle of human excellence. In contrast to our modern society which values, and even demands, increasingly narrow (and early) concentrations in educational and career tracks, Elizabethan society recognized and encouraged man's limitless potential for knowledge across a broad spectrum of disciplines and talents. In today's climate of super-specialization, the quest for well-roundedness might seem antiquated and antithetical. But at the center of Tudor court life, Queen Elizabeth, a remarkably talented linguist, writer, musician, dancer, athlete, and stateswoman, served as the pivotal role model for her courtiers, who sought to emulate her astonishing array of diverse interests and accomplishments. Through her personal example and demanding standards, Queen Elizabeth set the stage for the extraordinarily rich artistic and intellectual climate that enlivened the English court during the latter half of the sixteenth century.

As both a man and artist, Shakespeare was one of his society's most fully realized holistic products. Written in an era before access to dictionaries, glossaries, and Internet search engines, his plays reveal an exceptional command of vocabulary and a familiarity with an astonishing breadth of subjects, ranging from horticulture to seamanship to the law that can only be the product of wide reading and insatiable curiosity. His career accomplishments exemplify genuine integration of high artistry and high intellect. In his professional life, Shakespeare not only wrote plays, he acted in them, and may have had a hand in their direction. He was an astute businessman and investor, retiring as one of the wealthiest citizens of his native

Stratford-upon-Avon. Ironically, early in his career, Shakespeare's multifaceted talents even attracted the jealousy of rival playwright Robert Greene, who famously disparaged Shakespeare as a "Johannes factotum," or Jack of all trades. (It is worth noting, however, that Greene's slighting comments seem to arise primarily from educational elitism; he was a member of the so-called University Wits, a small group of university-educated dramatists, and was apparently stung by the public notice being paid to this less-educated newcomer from the country. Greene's publisher later apologized for his comments.)

Alongside the ideal of personal wholeness that Shakespeare personified, universal INTERCONNECTIVITY was a central preoccupation of Renaissance thinkers. Writing in the mid-twentieth century, the scholars E. M. W. Tillyard and A. O. Lovejoy concluded that Renaissance society was ordered in the concept of a hierarchical universe with God as its divine architect. According to this theory, Shakespeare's contemporaries found beauty, balance, and fitness in the logical orderliness of existence, which they attributed to the hand of God. They believed that discrete parts of the cosmos could only be fully understood by studying their relationship to other components of the universe, and by discovering affinities in dissimilarities. This penchant for exploring interlinkages was illustrated in the Great Chain of Being, which Lovejoy and Tillyard proposed as one of the most enduring cosmological metaphors of the medieval and Renaissance periods, exerting an inestimable influence on literature, visual art, politics, metaphysics, and philosophy. (By the late-twentieth century, with the advent of new historicism, gender studies, Marxist criticism, and a host of other scholarly perspectives, many scholars dismissed Tillyard and Lovejoy's conclusions as overly simplistic. Nevertheless, despite charges of datedness, they remain a crucial foundational component of the history of ideas, and an invaluable adjunct to the examination of status, alliance, and identity during the period.)

The concept of the Great Chain of Being arose from the premise that all living creatures and inanimate objects occupied a preordained hierarchical position on a natural ladder. At the top of the ladder was God. Descending vertically, angels inhabited the rungs closest to God, since they possessed the highest concentration of spirit. At the bottom of the ladder, rocks and other inanimate objects had their assigned places, since they lacked feelings, soul, or intellect. Plants, living but insensate, were positioned just above nonliving objects, followed by animals, which were more closely aligned with the region of matter than spirit. Man occupied a unique position in the middle of the ladder, balanced between the realms of pure animal and pure spirit. Capable of reason and the ability to impose order on his environment through the use of language, man possessed a soul that set him above and apart from other animals, yet he remained connected to his animal impulses through his physical appetites and senses.

Any disruption in the calm stability of the Great Chain of Being reverberated all along its length. A weakened link near the top of the chain imperiled all the rungs below; since any agitation could have disastrous consequences for the totality of the chain, each rung was both dependent on those above and responsible for those below. In *Troilus and Cressida*, Shakespeare references the natural ladder as a cosmic stabilizer, a finely tuned string upon which cosmic harmony depends:

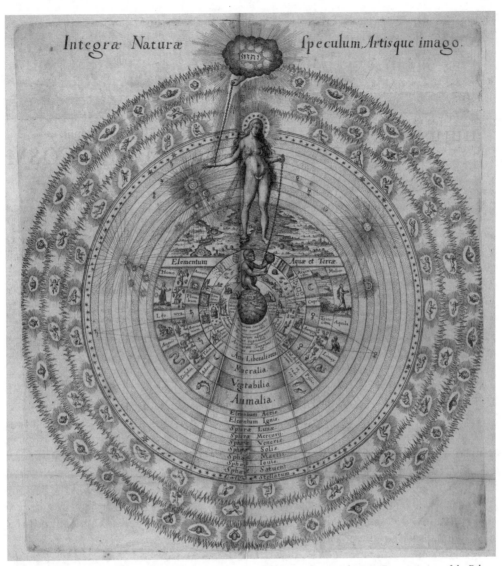

Depiction of the Great Chain of Being from Robert Fludd's 1617 *Utriusque cosmic-historia*. By permission of the Folger Shakespeare Library.

The heavens themselves, the planets, and this centre
Observe degree, priority, and place....
... But when the planets
In evil mixture to disorder wander,

What plagues and what portents, what mutiny!
... O, when degree is shak'd,
Which is the ladder of all high designs,
Then enterprise is sick. How could communities,
Degrees in schools, and brotherhoods in cities,
Peaceful commerce from dividable shores,
The primogenitive and due of birth,
Prerogative of age, crowns, sceptres, laurels,
But by degree stand in authentic place?
Take but degree away, untune that string,
And, hark, what discord follows!
(*Troilus and Cressida, I, iii, 85–6, 94–6, 101–10*)

While the Great Chain of Being reinforced Renaissance ideas about the fixedness of social status (a notion appropriately abandoned in modern civilization), it also served as an influential cultural metaphor that advanced awareness of continuity and communal responsibility, two foundational tenets of modern holistic thought. Every member of Elizabethan society was aware of both his/her dependence on and responsibilities to other people. Today, the chain provides an insightful resource for enlightening modern students about the power structures that underscore every Shakespearean play, provoking conversation and consideration of relationships and social dynamics and expressing the values of community and connectedness embedded in the holistic mentality.

Analogical thinking comprised the dominant cognitive mode of the Renaissance period. Using the analogical method, learners gain insights by comparing new information with familiar concepts through the recognition of patterns and similarities. In contrast, current educational models tend to emphasize atomistic or mechanistic thinking that divides subject matter into parts, often with little reference to the whole. One familiar example of analogical cognition is exemplified by the Renaissance doctrine of correspondences, which contended that just as God governed the angels, the king was head and ruler of men, and the lion the king of beasts (Tillyard 1961). This penchant for discovering analogies or correspondences was a definitive element of Renaissance thought and remains one of the most powerful instructional tools for the holistic Shakespeare teacher.

A significant example of correspondence is illustrated by contemporary perceptions of the human body, which was regarded as a "small world," or microcosm, a miniature replication of the "great universe," or macrocosm (Tillyard 1961). Perfect and beautiful in its composition, the human body mirrored in its structure, organs, and natural processes a variety of corollary cycles and systems, ranging from the passage of the seasons to the movement of the planets. Belief in embodied emotion, a further outgrowth of the concept of correspondence, comprised another of the seminal axioms of Renaissance medicine and anatomy. Based on Greek medical theory, the principle of emotional EMBODIMENT was rooted in the presumption that human passions are both situational and organic; that is,

1574 engraving depicting the humours. The Four Humours, from 'Quinta Essentia' by Leonhart Thurneisser zun Thurn (1531–95/6) published in Leipzig, 1574 (engraving) (b/w photo) by German School, (sixteenth century) Private Collection/ Archives Charmet/ The Bridgeman Art Library.

they may be provoked either by traumatic life events or by constitutional imbalances caused by humors, bodily fluids produced by the liver, spleen, lungs, and gall bladder (Paster 2004). When the humors were in appropriate balance, medical practitioners believed, a patient's temperament and mood were moderate and controlled. However, during times of illness or stress, excessive production of one or more of the humors caused noxious gases to travel to the patient's brain, causing emotional disturbances that required medical intervention, such as blood-letting or the administration of purgatives. Disruption of the unity and harmonious functioning of the body might also be triggered by societal or cosmic unrest and vice versa. In *King Lear*, for example, the aging king's mental deterioration is paralleled by unusual climatic events, such as storms and eclipses. Thus, Shakespeare's plays provide a rich mine for renewing awareness and contemplation of the symbiotic relationship between body, mind, spirit, and environment.

Shakespeare's Education

Although no records have survived that document Shakespeare's school enrollment, as the son of a local official, Shakespeare was entitled to free education at his local grammar school. By Shakespeare's schooldays the Tudor educational system had undergone reforms aimed at establishing a standard curriculum to ensure that all Protestants could read the Bible. Roger Ashcam, the highly regarded tutor of Elizabeth I, detailed a new, progressive instructional model in his book *The Scholemaster*, in which he extolled gentle correction and a collaborative relationship between student and instructor. Praise, mutual respect, and interactivity were keynotes of Ascham's teaching model, with focus placed on the instructor's role as facilitator and encourager of student learning: "This is a lively and perfect way of teaching of [linguistic] rules; where the common way, used in common schools, to read the grammar alone by itself, is tedious for the master, hard for the scholar, cold and uncomfortable for them both" (quoted in McDonald 2001, p. 66).

Although many negative elements of the Tudor educational model, such as the widespread practices of caning and other forms of corporal discipline, insistence on rote repetition and memorization, and the demand for unquestioning obedience to the schoolmaster are at stark odds with the aims of holistic education, a couple of beneficial attributes of Tudor schooling are worth noting as possible influences on Shakespeare's receptive imagination.

Content Immersion

At the King's New School, the Stratford-upon-Avon grammar school that Shakespeare likely attended throughout his boyhood, the curriculum centered on classical literature written in Latin, the universal language of the educated and literary elite. A series of Oxford-educated schoolmasters likely ensured a high instructional standard. Schoolmasters relied on a fusion of teaching strategies to enhance linguistic fluency. At most schools, in the upper levels, all instruction and conversation was conducted in Latin; language immersion encouraged the mastery of the varied and complex grammar and syntax of the foreign language, while exploiting the social community of the classroom to promote personal language development. Students were required not just to understand content in the foreign language but also to apply it in everyday conversations, situations, and relationships. Notwithstanding Ben Jonson's slighting reference to Shakespeare's "small Latine and lesse Greeke," the playwright's daily immersion in the Latin language during his formative years fostered a lifelong appreciation for the culture, literature, and languages of the classical era that deeply informed his invention of plots, use of rhetoric, and the metrical structures he employed in his playwriting.

Double translation of Latin verse, a classroom activity used for enhancing linguistic proficiency, exemplified one methodology of linguistic instruction used by some schoolmasters (McDonald 2001, p. 44). A favorite exercise of Roger Ascham, this activity required the instructor to read aloud an unfamiliar verse passage in Latin to his students. Students were expected to listen attentively and then write a literal translation of the Latin text in English. Next, they were asked to translate their English version back into well-constructed Latin verse that closely approximated the original. (This typical classroom exercise is dramatized in the language lesson scene of *The Merry Wives of Windsor*, when the Welsh parson, Sir Hugh Evans, quizzes a young scholar, appropriately named William, about the dual translation of the word "lapis." Their language lesson descends into farce when the uneducated Mistress Quickly mistakes their conversation for bawdy sexual innuendo.)

Memorization, cognition, and accuracy were used as avenues to encourage student progression from imitation to original creative writing. As students became increasingly proficient in Latin, they were allowed to script their own original dialogue and craft rhetorical arguments to supplement the texts they studied. They also took part in schoolhouse performances of both classical plays and works written in imitation of Latin and Greek sources. Such increasingly proactive, student-driven learning techniques are hallmarks of the modern holistic educational model. It is also notable that Tudor methods of teaching linguistic mastery were grounded in progressive integration of literary and theatre-centered activities, which are frequently polarized in modern classrooms. In the holistic Shakespeare classroom, the plays' primary intended function as performance scripts should remain a central focus. Through application of theatre-based exercises, learning becomes active, kinesthetic, and exploratory, promoting collaboration and shared discoveries.

Mixed-Ability Learning Groups

Classroom organization in the Elizabethan classroom is also of interest to the modern holistic teacher. In contrast to the homogeneous stratification of many modern classrooms, the standard upper level Elizabethan classroom comprised a diverse student body of varied ages (around 10–14) and multiple ability levels. Such mixed groupings have been shown to have a profound positive influence on peer mentoring and cooperative learning, while inhibiting negative stereotyping and static development. Students in multiage, multiability classrooms benefit from peer encouragement and shared interaction with learners of differing developmental stages. More advanced students develop leadership skills and confidence through their achievements, while younger students are motivated by the encouragement and example of their higher-level peers. In the holistic Shakespeare classroom, heterogeneous classroom populations can provoke a more lively and cooperative learning environment.

The Splintered Actor

Without question, Shakespeare's genius makes extraordinary demands on the modern student who strives to emulate the playwright's intellectual and intuitive synergy. However, an analogy from the rehearsal room illustrates the pitfalls of trying to confine Shakespeare's genius within narrow boundaries. One of the major challenges that confront the modern Shakespearean actor is the fragmentation of mind, body, and emotion that infects much classical performance. The density of Shakespeare's text and the need to puzzle through the complexities of rhythm and language often cause the actor to become locked in the cerebral and technical, while losing touch with the organic and emotional. Focused on textual excavation, the Shakespearean actor faces the danger of becoming (like Coleridge's apt description of Hamlet) a victim of excessive contemplation. The result is "talking head" acting, with performers concentrating on the intellectual journey that is one delight of Shakespearean performance, but neglecting the visceral and emotional voyage that is essential to fully dimensional acting. Although the performance of the overly cerebral actor might be clearly reasoned and technically precise, it feels empty and detached, leaving the audience dissatisfied and unmoved. Equally problematic is the actor whose performance is built exclusively on intuition and emotion. Motivated by concerns that analytical work might straitjacket creativity and spontaneity, the emotional actor consciously avoids the detailed technical work that would lend form and structure to his performance. Focused predominantly on his internal journey, this actor fails to clearly shape Shakespeare's rhetorical arguments or give voice to the poetic lyricism of Shakespeare's language, with the result that his performance, while dynamic and exciting to watch, is ultimately more focused on the actor's process than its reception and understanding by the audience. Just as the cerebral actor's performance seems hollow and incomplete, the emotion-centered actor delivers a fragmentary portrayal of his character, substituting sound and fury for substance. Such truncated performance choices make it impossible for Shakespeare's roles to emerge as fully realized portraits of humanity.

These splintered actors are locked into self-limiting modes of work that inhibit fully expressive performance. They lack confidence to tap into the power of a wholly invested portrayal, one that utilizes the sum total of their intellectual, emotional, and spiritual selves. Consequently, they are forever performing in half-light, leaving much of their artistic potential shadowed and concealed. Similarly, students of Shakespeare, whether in the theatre or literary classroom, require skillful direction and encouragement to use the resources of the whole body/mind/spirit to achieve their deepest and most satisfying personal encounter with Shakespeare. The learning modules detailed in the next four chapters will serve as exemplars toward a more integrated, student-centered holistic teaching method.

Chapter 2

Stages of Green: *A Midsummer Night's Dream*

The lunatic, the lover, and the poet
Are of imagination all compact . . .
And as imagination bodies forth
The forms of things unknown, the poet's pen
Turns them to shapes, and gives to aery nothing
A local habitation and a name.
(MSND V.i. 7–8, 14–17)

Perhaps no play more fully expresses Shakespeare's appreciation for his natural environment than his masterful comedy, *A Midsummer Night's Dream*. Set in an enchanted wood outside Athens, the play contrasts the repressive patriarchy of the court of Duke Theseus, with its formalized protocol, inflexible laws, and fixed social hierarchy, with the alternate reality of the fairies' moonlit otherworld, a space of freedom, magic, and rapturous discovery. Shakespeare uses the play's lush pastoral landscape as a central metaphor symbolizing personal transformation and regeneration, healing and spiritual renewal.

The Edenic setting of *A Midsummer Night's Dream* offers abundant opportunities for consideration of our relationship with and responsibilities to the natural world. Through its two mirror societies, the restrictive Athenian court and the magical fairy kingdom, the play explores the complementary relationship between urban and natural environments and the necessity for their harmonious co-existence. It invites students to consider the significance of organic spaces in their own lives and reflect on the fundamental connections between personal behaviors and ecological well-being. This chapter outlines strategies for teaching *A Midsummer Night's Dream* as both a theatrical text and as an avenue for provoking thought about each individual's role in ensuring environmental stability in the modern world. Students will study the play from historical, critical, and theatrical perspectives, with particular attention paid to the play's treatment of nature and environment.

Background and Context: The Green World of *A Midsummer Night's Dream*

In his book, *A Natural Perspective*, Canadian literary critic Northrup Frye identifies *A Midsummer Night's Dream* as one of Shakespeare's "green world" plays. Frye borrowed the phrase from the First Stanza of John Keats's poem *Endymion*:

A thing of beauty is a joy for ever:
Its loveliness increases; it will never
Pass into nothingness; but still will keep
A bower quiet for us, and a sleep
Full of sweet dreams, and health, and quiet breathing.
. . . Such the sun, the moon,
Trees old and young, sprouting a shady boon
For simple sheep; and such are daffodils
With the green world they live in. . . .

Frye adopts Keats's phrase "green world" to describe a set of comedies and romances, including *As You Like It* and *A Midsummer Night's Dream*, that follow a distinctive structural pattern. The green world plays begin in a conventional, rule-bound society dominated by older authority figures. Intergenerational conflict arises when the parental figures obstruct the romantic and personal choices of the youthful heroes, forcing the lovers to flee the strictures of civilization and seek refuge in a dream-like natural environment, a place of wonder, imagination, and innocence. This alternate space offers both an exile and a haven, a place of escape and reprieve, where man-made order gives place to natural order, and contemplation, music, poetry, and imagination supplant societal conformity. In this idyllic oasis, the young protagonist undergoes a spiritual journey toward self-knowledge, for it is a place that makes exploration of personal identity, artistic expression, and experimentation possible. Deep human relationships are forged in the quiet harbor of the green world; it is a removed space where spiritual regeneration heals fractured relationships, where the young are free to gratify their senses and follow the promptings of their hearts.

In *A Midsummer Night's Dream*, the play's three major plot lines are set in the environ of the mysterious, supernatural woods. For the mortal city-dwellers, this alien green world figures as a restorative, healing locale, a place for the temporary suspension of everyday cares. But while the urgent concerns and restrictive codes of behavior of the abandoned society are temporarily laid aside, connections with the conventional world are never fully severed. By the play's end, reconciliation between generations is achieved, harmony is restored, and the young characters return to their normal—though altered—lives in the city, to assume their positions within a newly minted social order in which power has passed to the next generation. At their core, the green world plays contain a rebellious impulse, since they advance a revisionist worldview in which the prevailing social hierarchy is subverted and the traditional authority of age is displaced by youth.

Contradiction lends another dimension to the environment of the green world, for this paradise is not without menace. In *A Midsummer Night's Dream*, strange creatures, both natural and supernatural, inhabit the woodland pathways of the magical forest. As the lovers enter the nighttime woods, landmarks are forgotten, friendships challenged, and social norms abandoned. Within this deceptive oasis, reality is suspended and magic rules. The implausible becomes plausible; Titania falls in love with an ass; the unpopular Helena suddenly finds herself the object of ardent pursuit by both Demetrius and Lysander. The mischievous Puck torments and teases the frightened mortals as they traverse through an alien nightscape where the boundaries between dream and nightmare, illusion and reality, are blurred. Disorientation amplifies their confusion and fear, conflict is heightened, and each member of the foursome feels isolated and distrustful of former alliances. Like Lewis Carroll's Alice, each human character undergoes a painful metamorphosis, a process of personal growth and self-analysis, as they learn the "rules" of their new environment, negotiate unforeseen challenges, and adapt to an altered reality. Lost in their strange new world, the young lovers must let go of fixed expectations and give in to the thrill and terror of the unknown. At the play's end, the matured characters emerge from the forest to assume their adult responsibilities in the City environment, newly committed to their altered roles and relationships.

The pastoral wonderland of *A Midsummer Night's Dream* reminds us of the regenerative spiritual power of green spaces. In the following modules, students will focus on specific topics relating to ecology or dramatic locale and then engage in practical activities that reinforce the significance of place in the play, in their personal lives, and in the global community.

Module #1

Ecological Themes in the *Dream*

Although no records survive that document the play's first performance, historians speculate that Shakespeare wrote *A Midsummer Night's Dream* as a masque for a lavish, aristocratic wedding around 1595. Certainly, with its theme of the triumph of young love over parental opposition and its fantasy setting of magical enchantment and nocturnal revelry, this celebratory play seems ideally suited for a marriage festivity. The plot is built around three convergent storylines which are conjoined by a subplot involving preparations for the upcoming nuptials of Duke Theseus, ruler of Athens, and his warrior bride Hippolyta:

- Two young lovers, Hermia and Lysander, run away from Athens when Hermia's father opposes their marriage and are pursued through a magical forest by their friends and rivals, Helena and Demetrius.

- Led by Bottom the weaver, a band of amateur performers, who work as laborers by day, meet in the woods to rehearse a play.

- Oberon and Titania, King and Queen of the fairies, quarrel over the custody of a changeling boy and entangle the bewildered mortals in their power struggle.

All three plots hinge on the characters' adventures in an untamed woodland, the mysterious habitat of the fairies. This fantasy location both parallels and contradicts the environment of Theseus's court, where in the first scene, Hermia is threatened with execution for refusing her father's choice of husband. Confronted with this show of brute force, the audience's assumptions about the civility of the Athenian court collapses and the play's dramatic conflict is set in motion. Beneath the reasonable and orderly facade of life in Athens, the seat of Western culture, barbaric laws hold sway.

In *A Midsummer Night's Dream*, Shakespeare continually reinforces the interdependence of its two locales, and by extension, implies their inhabitants' mutual responsibility for the health and harmony of their planet. Whatever threatens one world threatens both. The lovers' transition from known world to unknown world, from familiar, though inhibiting order to expressive personal freedom, is not without menace. Although Hermia and Lysander find temporary respite from the rigid civil and parental law of the City, they enter a world of parallel chaos, because the Fairyland is in the grips of its own catastrophe that has the potential to wreak death and destruction on the mortal world. Marital discord between the rulers of the fairy world has destabilized the ecosystem, threatening the homelands of both supernatural and mortal characters.

Ecological Crisis in Tudor/Stuart England

The play's preoccupation with ecological crisis reflects real-life environmental concerns that occupied public attention around the time of the play's composition. *A Midsummer Night's Dream* was written during a period of radical environmental change that threatened the economic stability of many rural communities and forever altered the face of the English countryside (Thirsk 1959). During Shakespeare's lifetime, two controversial economic and environmental topics, enclosure and deforestation, sparked tensions between the needs and wants of individuals and the rights of the larger community. These contemporary debates underscore the storyline and dual settings of *A Midsummer Night's Dream*. Today, the environmental concerns that Shakespeare voices in the play still resonate, as man's encroachment on and spoliation of the natural landscape continue to accelerate. The play serves as a timely reminder of our responsibility to serve as ethical stewards of the natural resources in our care.

During the late sixteenth century, a sharp rise in the practice of enclosure posed a dire economic threat to many farming communities. In accordance with ancient feudal custom, in most rural areas, open fields were available for communal use by small farmers. Enclosure marked a significant shift in these traditional land use practices, as the "commons" were fenced for grazing in response to the burgeoning wool trade, increasing profitability for the landowner, but removing the source of livelihood for farmers and displacing many poor cottagers. Protests against enclosure began in the mid-1590s, around the time of the composition of *A Midsummer Night's Dream* and gained intensity over the next two decades.

Economic stresses during these years were compounded by a series of disastrous harvests precipitated by bad weather, which caused widespread poverty and famine. The resulting social unrest caused by these man-made and climatic crises provides the darker context behind the play's light-hearted veneer.

In *A Midsummer Night's Dream*, the dense woods represent a mysterious place of magic and possibility. During the Tudor period, the depletion of this valuable resource exemplified a fundamental conflict between human needs and man's ethical responsibility to safeguard the integrity of natural resources. Deforestation posed a pressing environmental challenge during the Tudor era. The countryside surrounding Stratford had once been a heavily forested, undeveloped space, providing a free refuge for the homeless, a recreational haven for the privileged, and a natural habitat for animals and plants. During the Middle Ages, the Forest of Arden, a largely unspoiled natural territory through which no roads trespassed, covered the area north of Stratford. Since Shakespeare's maternal ancestors, the Ardens, had lived in this region for many years, during his boyhood in Stratford, Shakespeare likely heard descriptions that were handed down through the generations of the once nearly impenetrable woods. However, because the Arden Forest did not fit strict legal definitions, it was unprotected by Forest Law, which prohibited clearance and poaching. By Shakespeare's lifetime, the vast untamed spaces of the Warwickshire forests had been virtually lost.

Extension

Staging a Green Dream

With its ecological motifs, *A Midsummer Night's Dream* provides an ideal resource for teaching students about the principles of Green Theatre. Staging a theatre production requires considerable resources, many of which are thrown away after the show closes. During the past decade, the Green Theatre movement has grown from a small grassroots initiative into a nationwide enterprise that extends into the commercial heart of American theatre, Broadway. Green Theatre has two principal aims: to encourage the use of environmentally friendly materials and methods to create theatre; and to use theatre as a means of teaching the importance of conservation, preservation, and sustainability issues, and for promoting consciousness of the climate crisis.

The quest for a greener theatre has spurred many innovations in recent years, for example in 2004, Earth Matters on Stage (EMOS) launched its first Ecodrama Playwrights Festival at the University of Oregon to encourage dramatists to write new plays that explore environmental issues. The annual ten-day festival attracts theatre artists and academics from around the world that share a desire to use the theatre as a vehicle for positive environmental action.

Broadway has also taken positive steps toward developing more eco-friendly theatre. The Broadway Green Alliance was formed in 2008 as a committee of the Broadway League.

It sponsors e-waste drives, collecting unused computers, cell phone, and other electronic devices from New York theatres for recycling and publishes an industry newsletter that encourages and chronicles the efforts of commercial theatres to be more environmentally minded. Many Broadway shows also now appoint Green Captains to spearhead company efforts to reduce their carbon footprint. In March 2009, Broadway's famed marquee lights went dark for one hour, joining the Las Vegas strip and national landmarks like the Empire State Building and Mount Rushmore in a national recognition of Earth Hour. That event raised industry awareness of Broadway's massive energy consumption, spurring many Broadway theatres to substitute more energy efficient bulbs for traditional marquee lights.

Established in 2000, London's Acola Theatre is also committed to becoming the world's first carbon neutral theatre. Located in a diverse, multicultural community in east London, the theatre's progressive environmental policies encompass virtually all aspects of its programming. Acola incorporates environmentally conscious policies into every phase of its administration and production planning and sponsors eco-friendly outreach projects,

The Willow Globe Theatre in Wales, a miniature replica of the Globe Theatre constructed entirely of natural willow. Courtesy of the Willow Globe.

including swap meets for trading usable clothing, book fairs, and educational lectures, demonstrations, and workshops.

Similarly, the Willow Globe Theatre in Wales, home of the classical theatre company Shakespeare Link, is an outdoor performance space constructed from all-organic materials. Instead of walls, the theatre features an open-frame made entirely of locally grown willow. A windmill and solar panels generate sufficient energy to fuel all the electrical needs of the facility and its productions.

Finally, in 2009, the critically renowned Aquila Theatre Company mounted an all-green tour of Henrik Ibsen's classic play, *An Enemy of the People*. Written in 1882, Ibsen's play concerns a doctor's efforts to bring attention to the contamination of the local water supply and the opposition he faces from townspeople reluctant to change their lifestyles and beliefs. The tour attempted to make the smallest possible impact on the environment by using second-hand materials to produce costumes, props, and sets, and reducing the electrical needs of the production by laying a reflective floor cloth on the stage floor and moving lighting instruments closer to the actors. The company also held post-show discussions with the audience to encourage on-going consideration of eco-issues and solicit community advice about how to further green the tour.

For the following activity, students will work in small groups to conceptualize a "green" approach to a hypothetical production of *A Midsummer Night's Dream*. The group will strive to come up with environmentally friendly solutions for every aspect of the production from backstage to front of house.

Each group member will assume one of the jobs that make up a collaborative artistic team: producer, designer(s), dramaturg, director, stage manager. The team's first task is to research the specific function and responsibilities of each job. It will quickly become evident that there are significant areas of overlap between many theatre positions. These shared boundaries reinforce the collaborative decision-making dynamic that is central to any production team. The exercise will also require participants to research materials and techniques used in set and costume construction and lighting.

As the team works together to develop a production approach to *A Midsummer Night's Dream* that employs green theatre techniques, they might consider some of these suggestions:

- Solicit found materials instead of constructing or purchasing new objects, thereby reducing waste and depletion of resources

- Seek out sustainable fabrics and building materials

- Use non-toxic paints and low-pollutant dyes

- Substitute energy efficient light sources

- Consider how paper can be eliminated or recycled

- Think about the life cycle of every material used in the production

- Educate the audience about the importance and health benefits of sustainability and environmental responsibility

- Create meaningful opportunities for outreach, such as community service projects that make a positive impact on the local or global community

Reflection

1. Explore the concept of "third places," significant locations outside home or work environments that serve as informal social gathering places that enrich the life of the community. In some neighborhoods, playhouses function as vibrant third places, providing integral locations for the exchange of ideas, and social, political, and creative interaction. In other communities, theatre facilities are viewed as formal, elitist spaces that exist for a privileged subset of society. How might administrators of local theatres develop plans to make theatre venues essential "third places" in community life?

2. Does theatre have a moral responsibility to educate audiences about important social or environmental issues? How might theatre administrators balance entertainment and social agendas?

Module #2

Shakespeare's Eden

Although many details about Shakespeare's biography remain shrouded in mystery, one thing is certain: he loved and understood nature. His plays make that fact abundantly obvious. Despite economic realities and the demands of a profession that transplanted Shakespeare from his native Warwickshire to urban London by his late twenties, throughout his lifetime, the dramatist remained deeply tied to his roots in the English West Country. As a boy in Stratford-upon-Avon, a prosperous market town approximately 100 miles northwest of London, outdoor life would have dominated young William's everyday activities whenever he was free of the enclosed walls of the classroom. Throughout his childhood, Shakespeare probably regularly made the three-mile trek through the countryside to visit his Arden relatives on their farm in Wilmcote. During later youth, his wanderings led him in the direction of nearby Shottery to court his sweetheart Anne Hathaway, a farmer's daughter. In the years following his marriage, he joined a troupe of actors that annually crisscrossed the English provinces, either on foot or by cart, taking refuge during the hot summer months from the ever-present threat of plague in the overcrowded city of London. Shakespeare's extensive travels as an itinerant actor brought him into encounter with both carefully sculpted, formal gardens in the stately homes where he performed and with the untamed wildflowers and hedgerows that lushly populated the English countryside; in his plays, he writes lyrically and descriptively about both types of natural settings. Near the end of his life, after years of success in the city as the preeminent playwright of his day, Shakespeare retired to the bucolic tranquility of his hometown. There, his passion for nature was perhaps shared through conversation with his son-in-law, Dr. John Hall, a noted doctor and herbalist. Despite his professional triumphs within the most sophisticated urban culture of his day, Shakespeare remained at heart a man of the land throughout his life, and his plays attest to his enduring, passionate connection to the earth.

Shakespeare's abiding respect for his country heritage resonates as a recurrent motif in his thirty-eight plays, which contain references to nearly 200 plants and flora and reveal a countryman's intimate knowledge of a vast variety of botanicals. His plays illustrate Shakespeare's awareness of the medical uses of myriad herbs; they speak with the voice of authority and personal experience about methods of insect and weed control, planting, pruning, grafting, and fertilization, about growth patterns and the seasonal variations of the land. In his dramatic works, Shakespeare's keen observation of the world of nature combines with his gift for evocative description to provide an insightful guide to Renaissance horticulture. But Shakespeare's interest in nature goes beyond the prosaic. He was conversant in the symbology of plant life, which provides one of the most prolific sources of imagery in his dramatic writing. The hidden language of flowers figures prominently in many of his plays, most memorably in Ophelia's mad scene in *Hamlet*, in which she gives each character a flower whose symbolism embodies the recipient's behavior, morality, or state of mind. Throughout the Shakespearean canon, the playwright artfully employs the figurative meaning of plants and flowers as a dramatic device to reveal character and further plot.

In *A Midsummer Night's Dream*, Shakespeare indulges his passion for colorful descriptions of his natural world, celebrating the native English landscape that he loved. He uses luxuriant and sensual language to evoke a paradisiacal setting that needs no concrete illustration.

OBERON:

> I know a bank where the wild thyme blows,
> Where oxlips and the nodding violet grows,
> Quite over-canopied with luscious woodbine,
> With sweet musk-roses and with eglantine:
> There sleeps Titania sometime of the night,
> Lull'd in these flowers with dances and delight;
> And there the snake throws her enamell'd skin,
> Weed wide enough to wrap a fairy in. . . .
> (II. i. 249–56)

References to the animal kingdom form another key motif in Shakespeare's plays, which contain allusions to almost 200 types of animal and bird life, both real and mythical, ranging from the native creatures of the Stratford countryside—hedgehogs, deer, hares, owls, and larks—to foreign species, like the lion that frightens Thisby in *A Midsummer Night's Dream*'s play-within-the-play. In his writing, Shakespeare's faunal references, which include legendary creatures like unicorns and dragons, support dramatic situation and mood, frequently drawing correlations between animal habits and characteristics and those of their human counterparts.

A Midsummer Night's Dream abounds with evocative references to the beasts that share the forest with the fairies. The magic woods teem with nocturnal creatures, both benign and dangerous; these animals constitute an essential part of the play's mise en scene, adding dimension and detail to the fairy kingdom. Shakespeare even remembers the insects, worms, and other tiny critters that inhabit the forest floor of the fairyland. These smallest living things are addressed in the lullaby with which Titania's fairy attendants serenade their Queen as she settles down to sleep in her flowery bower:

> You spotted snakes with double tongue,
> Thorny hedgehogs, be not seen;
> Newts and blind-worms, do no wrong,
> Come not near our fairy queen.
> Philomel, with melody
> Sing in our sweet lullaby;

Lulla, lulla, lullaby, lulla, lulla, lullaby:
Never harm,
Nor spell nor charm,
Come our lovely lady nigh;
So, good night, with lullaby.
Weaving spiders, come not here;
Hence, you long-legg'd spinners, hence!
Beetles black, approach not near;
Worm nor snail, do no offence.
(2. 2. 9–23)

Shakespeare's love for his native rural heritage resonates throughout the plot and imagery of *A Midsummer Night's Dream*. His deep personal ties to the land inspired the play's sylvan setting and still speak of his intimate love for the place where he was reared.

Extension

Exploring Place, Memory, and Self-Identity

Our sense of place is intimately tied to our understanding of who we are and what makes us unique. Memories of the places that hold special meaning in our lives provide sturdy roots that connect us to those people with whom we share trusting relationships and a common heritage and enable us to maintain a strong self-image, even when the demands of modern life require us to journey far from the comfort of safe and familiar surroundings.

Life transitions are frequently accompanied by dislocation from the places we consider home. When ties to the places that we hold dear are disrupted, self-identity often undergoes a period of crisis or transformation. Separation from the places we cherish often goes hand in hand with distance from the people we love and loss of familiar routines. Whether dislocation involves young adults leaving the shelter of home and family to begin a new life on a college campus, or elderly relatives moving into assisted living, establishment of a new sense of place ownership is a necessary component of successful transition at every stage of life.

Although separated from his native region for most of his professional life, Shakespeare used memory and art to sustain his deep attachment to his rural origins, producing descriptive imagery to create lasting, vivid snapshots of the landscape he loved. Following his example, we can use both reflective activities and shared communication to keep connections to our significant spaces alive, renewing our sense of belonging and our confidence in where we come from and where we are going.

In the Place Memory Sonnet activity, students will recapture a meaningful place in their lives through a sonnet-writing exercise. The activity is divided into three parts: an analytical component, a reflective element, and a creative writing exercise. The latter activity will require students to work within a formalized literary form, while simultaneously engaging the powers of emotional and sensory recall.

Part I

Introduces students to the fundamental structure of a Shakespearean sonnet. This analytical section will establish the foundation for the creative writing exercise that follows.

Activity

- Using Sonnet 18, have students number the lines in the left margin from 1–14.

- Explain that the sonnet is organized into four quatrains and a final couplet. Have students label each quatrain (Q1–Q4). Ask them to notice that each quatrain develops a single idea, and that transitions in thought are marked by introduction of a new quatrain.

- Point out that the sonnet adopts a clear rhyme pattern: ABABCDCDEFEFGG. Direct students to copy this rhyme key in the right margin of the sonnet as indicated below.

- Explain the basic structure of iambic pentameter, noting that each verse line contains 5 pairs of syllables, with the first syllable possessing a soft stress and the second a strong stress.

- Ask students to place a hand on the pulse of his/her throat to feel the surge of the blood flow in their veins. This will demonstrate that iambic pentatmeter is a highly organic rhythmic form, since it echoes the sound of the human heart.

- Have students divide each verse line into feet (or pairs of syllables) as illustrated.

1. Shall I | compare | thee to | a sum | mer's day? A
2. Thou art | more love | ly and | more tem | perate. B
3. Rough winds | do shake | the dar | ling buds | of May, A
4. And sum | mer's lease | hath all | too short | a date. B

5. Sometime | too hot | the eye | of heav | en shines, C
6. And of | ten is | his gold | complex | ion dimmed, D

7. And ev | ery fair | from fair | sometime | declines, C
8. By chance, | or na | ture's chang | ing course, | untrimmed. D

9. But thy | eter | nal sum | | mer shall | not fade, E
10. Nor lose | posses | sion of | that fair | thou ow'st, F
11. Nor shall | Death brag | thou wand' | rest in | his shade, E
12. When in | eter | nal lines | to time | thou grow'st. F

13. So long | as men | can breathe | or eyes | can see, G
14. So long | lives this, | and this | gives life | to thee. G

Part II

Of the exercise commences with a simple breathing exercise designed to promote relaxation and inner reflection.

Activity

- Students lie on their backs with their eyes closed in a dim, distraction-free space. Using a calm, unhurried voice, the facilitator guides the students through a personal inventory of body tension. Beginning at the feet and traveling upward to the head, students are asked to focus on each area of the body, checking for unconscious tension. If tension is detected, students gently self-correct by mentally directing muscles in that area to release.

- Next, the facilitator asks students to simply concentrate on their breathing. In relaxation and centering exercises, breath-holding is a common barrier to full release. Remind students to keep their jaws loose and slightly open and to continue breathing naturally. Once students have become aware of the inspiration and exhalation of their breath, ask them to release each exhalation on a soft "huh" sound. The sound should be light and unforced, produced by the slightest possible vocalization to accompany the release of breath. After 10 repetitions, change the sound to a hum, allowing the length of the vocalization to match the length of the natural breath. Again, no action should be forced or hurried.

- Once the class has become relaxed and centered on breath and inner reflection, ask students to cast their memories back to a place that holds strong positive associations. Encourage students to be as specific as possible in their selection of the place (the rocking chair on their grandparents' back porch, for example, instead of the general city or town where the house is located).

- Ask students to really "see" the space, tapping into the powerful potential of sense memory. Have the students visualize individual objects within the space, paying attention to small details, patterns, and colors.

- Students should gradually narrow their concentration onto a single object within the space. In their imagination, have them reach out and touch the object, tracing its lines, and remembering its size, weight, and texture. Ask them to notice whether the object has a particular smell and if it produces a sound when shaken or moved. Tell the students to imagine pressing their tongue to the object, detecting whether it has a distinctive taste.

- Encourage the students to open their eyes and slowly return to a sitting position. Be aware that this exercise may evoke strong emotional responses in some students. Allow students to experience whatever emotions might be stimulated, without directing unnecessary attention to individuals experiencing emotional releases.

Part III

Of the exercise progresses to creative writing.

Activity

- Students should record their recollections of the sense memory experience in a journal, carefully noting details of the sensory recall.

- Students will use their journal notes to write a sonnet about the object and its relevance to their significant space. They should adhere to the structure and structure of a Shakespearean sonnet, but personalize their poem by drawing on the emotional resonances evoked by the item.

- Finally, the sonnets will be shared with the class. Students will place their sonnets in a pile on the floor, without any identification affixed. Each student will randomly select a sonnet from the pile to read aloud to the class. Allow participants several minutes to familiarize themselves with the sonnet they have chosen, so that they are prepared to deliver the most effective possible reading of their peer's work.

Reflection

1. Did the formality of the sonnet structure limit or enhance your creative writing? Why? How did this affect your working process?

2. What did you remember or discover about your personal connections to a specific place?

3. How has your awareness of Shakespeare's connections to his native region enhanced your understanding or appreciation for *A Midsummer Night's Dream*?

Module #3

Discovering Character through Imagery and Place

In the 1970s, ecocriticism emerged as a new form of literary scholarship. By definition, ecocriticism is an interdisciplinary field of study that draws correlations between works of literature and the physical environment. Also called "green studies," ecocriticism developed in response to the rise of environmental ecology. This branch of literary criticism has gained prominence in recent years, as the technological age has generated increasing disconnection from our natural world.

Ecocriticism embraces a broad spectrum of Earth-centered topics and concerns. One central area of interest is the use of character to embody place. Literature contains many examples of human characters that personify the qualities of their environment.

In the popular children's book, *The Secret Garden* by Frances Hodgson Burnett, the essence of the English countryside is represented by the character of Dickon Sowerby, a Pan-like child of the land whose intimate understanding of plant life and animals helps two emotionally wounded children to heal. In this simple but uplifting story, an awkward, self-centered orphan girl named Mary Lennox learns to love and trust through her friendship with Dickon, who encourages her pleasure in gardening. Rejuvenated by her connections with Dickon and the earth, Mary shows another emotionally stunted child, the spoiled and sickly Colin Craven, the pathway to physical health and spiritual growth.

Emily Bronte captures the spirit of the wild, untamed English moors in her classic work, *Wuthering Heights*. The brooding, haunted Heathcliff characterizes the stark and stormy atmosphere of the northern landscape, which both attracts and repels the impulsive Catherine. Bronte contrasts descriptions of the gloomy, decaying Wuthering Heights with the elegant, light-filled manor house Thrushcross Grange, to parallel the appearance and personalities of Cathy's rival lovers, Heathcliff and Edgar Linton.

Sheila Callaghan employs an unusual but effective dramatic device in her 2004 play, *Crumble (Lay Me Down Justin Timberlake)*. In this play, the physical setting, a once grand but now dilapidated apartment, becomes an actual character. Portrayed as an embittered, down-at-heel gentleman, the apartment complains about its inhabitants' neglect as it bears witness to a mother and daughter's isolation from one another as they struggle to work through their grief following the accidental death of the father.

In *A Midsummer Night's Dream*, Titania serves as a personification of the natural world and as its central mother figure. In the fairyland, she is a protective, nurturing presence. However, Titania's maternal instincts toward a little Indian boy have brought the prospect of famine, disease, and death to the mortal world. Her adoption of the boy, the child of a devotee who died in childbirth, has enflamed the jealousy of Oberon, who has demanded custody of the child. The feud caused by Titania's refusal to yield up the little boy, combined with Oberon's rage over her doting attentions to the boy, has unleashed disastrous consequences beyond the marital sphere. Because of their symbiotic relationship with the natural environment, the quarrel between the fairy king and queen has destabilized the climate, generating toxic fogs and heavy rains. Waterlogged crops rot in the fields, affecting the food supply of the Athenians. The possibility of death for the innocent human population distresses Titania's motherly, feminine instincts, and she laments the imbalance caused by the rupture between the fairy couple:

TITANIA:

> These are the forgeries of jealousy;
> And never, since the middle summer's spring,
> Met we on hill, in dale, forest or mead,
> By paved fountain or by rushy brook,
> Or in the beached margent of the sea,
> To dance our ringlets to the whistling wind,
> But with thy brawls thou hast disturb'd our sport.
> Therefore the winds, piping to us in vain,
> As in revenge, have suck'd up from the sea
> Contagious fogs; which falling in the land,
> Hath every pelting river made so proud

That they have overborne their continents.
The ox hath therefore stretch'd his yoke in vain,
The ploughman lost his sweat, and the green corn
Hath rotted ere his youth attain'd a beard.
The fold stands empty in the drowned field,
And crows are fatted with the murrion flock;
The nine men's morris is fill'd up with mud,
And the quaint mazes in the wanton green,
For lack of tread, are undistinguishable.
The human mortals want their winter cheer;
No night is now with hymn or carol blest.
Therefore the moon (the governess of floods),
Pale in her anger, washes all the air,
That rheumatic diseases do abound.
And thorough this distemperature, we see
The seasons alter. Hoary-headed frosts
Fall in the fresh lap of the crimson rose,
And on old Hiems' thin and icy crown
An odorous chaplet of sweet summer buds
Is, as in mockery, set; the spring, the summer,
The childing autumn, angry winter, change
Their wonted liveries; and the mazed world,
By their increase, now knows not which is which.
And this same progeny of evils comes
From our debate, from our dissension;
We are their parents and original.
(II, i, 81–117)

Extension

Playing a Monologue with Specificity and Clarity

Titania's monologue exemplifies several very common acting challenges. The speech is essentially a long list, one of the most daunting forms of monologue. Unless the performer manages to capture the illusion that the items in the list are springing to mind naturally and spontaneously, any memorized list can quickly become monotonous. The speech is also full of lush imagery, which can lull the performer into a generalized "poetic" mood, unless the images are personal and specific. In rehearsal, the speech often suffers from the performer's reliance on over-lyricism, with the result that generalized mood subsumes meaning and clarity. Finally, the sheer length of the 37-line speech can be intimidating. To overcome this barrier, the performer needs to carve out the shape of the thought, while remaining ever-conscious of Titania's urgent need to speak in order to convince Oberon of the destructiveness of his anger.

Characters use language both to communicate their thoughts and feelings to other characters and the audience and to persuade others to change their own viewpoints and actions. This central desire for communication is often forgotten when preparing a speech of the length, complexity, and poetic richness of Titania's monologue. In the following exercise, students will break down the monologue to keep its descriptive imagery alive and highlight the tension and conflict of the scene's context.

Activity

- For this exercise, students should begin by sitting in a circle. Distribute a copy of Titania's monologue (printed above) to each student in the class.

- Start by having the class read the speech aloud in unison, with the simple aim of comprehending the meaning of the speech. Reading in unison will help eliminate self-consciousness and nervousness about reading in front of peers. After the first read-through, point out any words with difficult pronunciations and discuss terms with unclear or obscure meanings.

- Have students notice the final words of each verse line. These important words, which relate primarily to environment and emotion, essentially tell the whole story of the monologue. Next, ask students to read the first word in each line. The abundance of small connective words, such as "but" or "and," give the speech its build and impetus. The spilling deluge of language illustrates Titania's pressing desire to convince Oberon of his errors.

- Read the monologue through a second time. On this round, have individual students read until they reach a either a period or semi-colon, at which point, the next student in the circle should pick up the reading. There should be no pauses or hesitations between speakers. Instead, each student should attempt to build on the energy and fluidity of the previous speaker. This shared reading structure will allow students to experience the shape of Titania's thoughts, lending greater clarity to her speech.

- A third reading will focus on releasing the energy and mounting urgency of the speech. Students should stand shoulder to shoulder in a tight circle. They will read the monologue by short, individual phrases, moving to the next student on EVERY piece of punctuation, including commas. The distinctive vocal tones and rhythms of individual speakers will automatically lend the phrases greater specificity and color.

- Repeat the previous step to increase familiarity with the monologue. Make sure to begin with the same student, so that everyone 'owns' the same phrases as on the previous round.

- After this rotation, ask students to sit down in the circle, but to turn their backs to the group. Have them silently read through the monologue, remembering which of the descriptive phrases were theirs' during the last two readings. Once students have assembled their list of phrases, ask them to close their eyes and conjure up a specific, personal mental picture for each descriptive image.

- Ask student to rejoin the circle and again stand shoulder to shoulder. Once again, read the monologue aloud from phrase to phrase. As students speak their individual phrases, direct them to concentrate on their mental pictures. Much greater clarity and specificity of images that should result from this round.

- Next, have the students form Oberon/Titania pairs. Remind them that Titania's speech is the continuation of a long-running marital argument. Ask the students to stage the scene, focusing on the tensions between the two characters and the underlying conflict of the scene. Student will need to make decisions about blocking and stage business. For the performer playing Oberon, active listening is critical. What is Oberon doing during Titania's 37 line speech? Why does he not respond to her accusations or interrupt her long monologue? What actions might he perform that stimulate Titania to continue speaking?

- Present the scenes to the class. Follow the presentation with a talkback, asking students to share their discoveries about character, language, situation, and staging.

Module #4

Devising A Production Concept for A Midsummer Night's Dream

Throughout its performance history, *A Midsummer Night's Dream* has remained one of Shakespeare's most popular and accessible plays. Audience reception of the play has always been highly influenced by directorial concept and design choices, which serve as intermediaries between spectator and text. Directorial interpretation of place manipulates the ways in which we perceive and think about the play's complementary settings, and by extension, guides our responses to the play's themes, relationships, and values. Sometimes the director's approach to environment is deliberately at odds with the dramatist's intention, allowing us to see the play in a whole new way.

Like most Shakespearean texts, the script of *A Midsummer Night's Dream* contains only a handful of stage directions, leaving directors considerable artistic leverage to shape our responses through their visual aesthetic. When the play premiered in the late 16th Century, the original production likely used only a few simple set pieces to suggest its woodland setting. Spoken décor, rather than fully realized stage designs, suggested place. Although Shakespeare's theatre company, the Lord Chamberlain's Men (later the King's Men) owned its own permanent theatre, the Globe, where public performances were staged, the theatre building was an essentially neutral space. Only minimal furnishings and props were used to indicate changes in locale, or even to distinguish between the various plays in the company's repertoire. Shakespeare's acting troupe also toured extensively during the summer months and performed at private functions throughout the year. The diverse venues in which they played demanded considerable adaptability to spatial formations. Devoid of the visual embellishment of lavish stage settings, language and the audience's imagination became the scene designers.

The past hundred years have ushered in startlingly diverse directorial interpretations of the green world of *A Midsummer Night's Dream*. In the early twentieth century, English theatre actor and manager Herbert Beerbohm Tree staged a lavish production that exemplified Victorian tastes for sentimentality and spectacle. Intended to appeal to family audiences, the production transformed the theatre into a magnificent, whimsical dreamland where beautifully costumed children, their garments adorned by twinkling lights, portrayed sweet, ethereal fairies, and live rabbits scampered across a stage floor blanketed by blooming wild flowers and lush foliage. Tree's wondrous storybook rendering emphasized the gentleness and romance of the forest world, a fanciful realm of safety and playful innocence.

In 1914, Harley Granville-Barker abandoned illusionistic settings and focused instead on the primacy of the language. For his production of *A Midsummer Night's Dream*, Granville-Barker created an apron stage to enhance the proximity of spectator and performer and used curtains as his primary scenic element. His emphasis was on fast-paced action unhampered by cumbersome scene changes and on the actors' swift delivery of language.

Scene from Sir Herbert Beerbohm Tree's lavish 1900 production of *A Midsummer Night's Dream*. © Victoria and Albert Museum, London.

Granville-Barker's production inaugurated a dramatic reversal in the extravagant scenic practices of years past, stimulating fresh directorial experimentation.

In 1970, Peter Brook ripped away the play's sugarcoated veneer in a landmark production for the Royal Shakespeare Company. For his stripped down production, Brook employed metatheatrical devices that constantly reinforced the audiences' awareness that they were viewing a play, thus emphasizing the play's preoccupation with illusion. Designed by Sally Jacobs, a monochromatic white-walled box lit by stark light represented the moonlit woodland setting, its only splash of color provided by an enormous red feather that served as Titania's ultra-feminine flowery bower. An iron gallery surmounted the minimalist set and provided a vantage point from which various characters could observe the action below. Ladders and simple wire arches held by actors substituted for trees. To establish his vision of the play, Brook borrowed from the tricks and techniques of the circus: Oberon and Puck descended from the rafters on trapezes; the magic flower, love-in-idleness, became a silver plate spun on a stick;

Peter Brook's ground-breaking circus-inspired production, 1970. Tom Holte Theatre Photographic Collection © Shakespeare Birthplace Trust.

mounted on wooden stilts, an invisible Puck led Demetrius and Lysander on a frantic chase through the forest. Brook's simple but highly innovative staging garnered enormous critical and popular attention. It heralded a mass departure from pictorial realism, influencing a new generation of young directors who scrutinized and rejected the excessive ornamentation of earlier interpretations and abandoned saccharine readings of the play's themes.

The post-Brook years have marked a movement toward darker, more nightmarish interpretations of Shakespeare's fairy kingdom. In 1992, Canadian director Robert Lepage staged a photo-negative version of Brook's all-white production at the National Theatre. In place of Brook's white box, Lepage's fairyland became a mud-filled swamp through which the four lovers, dressed only in white nightclothes, trudged, becoming progressively disheveled and filthy. Gregory Doran's 2005 Goth-inspired production at the Royal Shakespeare Company was set in a sinister, metal-filled junkyard illuminated by a giant red moon. The fairies, costumed in a strange assortment of clothing items apparently scavenged from the piles of discarded objects that littered the stage, carried grotesque naked dolls reminiscent of the creepy toys that come alive in horror films. Doran's disturbing and vaguely malevolent fairies were the modern day reincarnation of the sprites of the Grimms' darkest tales. Obsessed by the human characters, they chased the young lovers through the woods, physically enacting the role of scenery by becoming bushes and thorny branches that literally tore the clothing from the frightened city-dwellers' backs.

Gregory Doran's Goth-influenced *Dream,* 2005. Stewart Hemley © Royal Shakespeare Company.

Effusive reviews greeted Tim Supple's visually stunning Anglo-Indian production of *A Midsummer Night's Dream* in 2006. The British Council originally commissioned this watershed reinterpretation of Shakespeare's classic play as a vehicle for cross-cultural exchange. It toured India and Sri Lanka and then played to sold-out audiences as part of the Royal Shakespeare Company's Complete Works Series in Stratford-upon-Avon. The international collaboration took two years to stage and featured the talents of actors, singers, musicians, and dancers assembled from across the Indian subcontinent. Working under the direction of Supple, a British director, a multilingual cast transcended language barriers to create a bold, eclectic fusion of noise and movement, more closely akin to the joyous chaos of a street festival than a conventional theatrical event. Highly saturated, jewel-like colors, astonishing athleticism, breathtaking visual spectacle, and exotic music served as the dominant theatrical media.

Each of the twenty-three performers spoke their lines in their native tongues, using eight different languages, including Tamil, Hindi, Sanskrit, Bengali, Sinhalese, Malayalam,

Marathi, and English. The cacophony of languages and dialects highlighted the difficulties of human communication, which became one of the production's major motifs. During the lovers' arguments, lines delivered in alternate languages served as an aural metaphor for the lovers' confusion, frustration, and miscommunication. Language, the star player in most Shakespearean productions, shared focus with a lush nonverbal soundscape, produced by chanting, song, and traditional Indian wind, string, and percussive musical instruments.

The production showcased the outstanding physicality of a diverse acting company drawn a patchwork of classical, street, and folk performance training backgrounds. The performers' mesmerizing physical skills included acrobatics, rope climbing, stick fighting, and traditional Indian dance forms, such as classical Bharatanatyam and Chhau, a type of tribal martial dance. Western-based and contemporary theatrical forms were also represented, resulting in a vibrant array of distinct performance styles.

In Supple's conception of Shakespeare's green world, the English woodland morphed into a dangerous jungle where the young lovers confronted forbidden appetites, taboos, and violent primal impulses, and shed their conventional City personas for alternate feral identities. Puck used giant rubber bands to entangle the lost lovers in a spider web that entrapped

Tim Supple's multi-lingual production for the RSC Complete Works 2006 season. Stewart Hemley © Royal Shakespeare Company.

the four friends. Caught in their dark but intoxicating new environment, the young lovers yielded to the indulgence of fierce sensuality and primitive, uninhibited desire.

Designer Sumant Jayakrishnan interpreted the play's green world as a jungle, using minimalist set pieces and a luxuriant palette of deep jewel tones. Red earth covered the stage floor, staining the actors' bare feet and costumes like dried blood. Festoons of red silk hangings cascaded from the fly space, providing a breathtaking vertical playing area. To create her bower, the actress playing Titania slithered up the silken fabric, and fashioned a makeshift cocoon where she remained suspended in mid-air. At the rear of the stage, a simple bamboo frame covered with paper served as the entry to the Fairyland and provided a device for characters to climb and perch. Following the opening scene, the fairies burst through the bamboo frame, tearing and shredding its paper cover, which littered the stage throughout the play, representing tangled underbrush and foliage. This dramatic entrance established the ephemeral separation between the worlds of reality and fantasy, safety and danger.

Extension

The Sensory Object Presentation

Dramatic texts are highly malleable works of literature, subject to reinterpretation by each new team of theatre artists. There is no definitive concept or setting for *A Midsummer Night's Dream*. In fact, as evidenced by his textual references to native English plants and animals, Shakespeare took significant dramatic license with the play's setting, creating a woodland oasis that more closely resembles rural Warwickshire than ancient Greece. Personal responses to a work of dramatic literature can evoke radically different stage interpretations of the play's setting and environment. Collaboration between director and designers allows each new artistic team to put its own interpretative signature on the world of the play.

In the months prior to rehearsals, the production team holds a series of talks to arrive at a conceptual approach to the play. Often, the director assumes primary responsibility for articulating the initial concept and guides the artistic team toward reaching a consensual production plan (although this process might be shared to greater or lesser degree, depending on the working methods of the company). The task of arriving at a production concept is both collaborative and contemplative, requiring individual artists to establish a strong identity with the play and communicate their personal vision to their peers.

Theatre artists often use sensory objects to express their emotional, spiritual, and intellectual responses to a play's environment, characters, and situation. For a director of *Macbeth*, for example, the sound of a baby rattle might be particularly evocative, establishing a powerful reminder of the play's references to absent babies and murdered children. Or the sharp smell of vinegar might provide a strong sensory reference for the actress playing Lady Macbeth, as she rehearses the monologue in which she asks supernatural powers to convert her mother's milk to gall, annihilating her feminine empathy.

Activity

For the Sensory Object Exercise

- Students begin by rereading the play individually, extracting five quotations that lend personal clarity to the play's setting, mood, or situation, that "speak" to the student about the world of the play.

- Using these five quotations as creative springboards, each student assembles a collection of objects that engage the senses. Students should be cautioned against privileging only the visual; taste, touch, smell, and hearing are equally powerful intuitive connectors. Allow the text to stimulate abstract free association, avoiding literal matching of word and object.

- Students come together in small groups to share their quotations and accompanying sensory objects. Participants should resist the impulse to *explain* the meaning of his/her objects, instead allowing peers to *experience* the objects, which may evoke highly varied emotional responses from each member of the group.

- After each group member has presented their objects and quotations, the students discuss the presentations, and consider the differing production approaches that might spring from each presentation.

Reflection

1. Consider a personal object that holds deep personal meaning in your life. How does the object reflect who you are? How do objects speak to our identity and bind us to place?

2. In a 2003 experiment, researchers at the University of Colorado at Boulder and Cornell University investigated the question: "Do experiences make people happier than material possessions?" (Boven 1193). Two groups of respondents were asked to consider their satisfaction with either a recent experiential or material expenditure for which they paid more than $100. Despite the relative durability of material goods compared to the ephemerality of experiential purchases, the group of participants rating experiential expenditures reported higher, more enduring satisfaction than other respondents. Why do you think about these results? What does this experiment reveal about the value of memories, as opposed to tangible items? What about the significance of souvenirs and personal keepsakes? If you were able to save one item during a disaster, what would it be? Why?

Module #5

Exploring Spatiality in Theatre

Students of Shakespeare usually study in sterile, climate-controlled classrooms, separated from each other by desks, and insulated from the ambient noises of the outdoors. In classroom settings, spatial configuration often tacitly reflects the philosophical underpinnings of the educational system. In some British universities, for example, the professor's desk or lectern is mounted higher than the students, providing a spatial metaphor for the classroom's unequal power structure. In sharp contrast, Montessori classrooms feature task-oriented workstations that allow the students to move freely around the room at his/her individual pace and choose to work on specific projects that engage their interest.

In the theatre, many directors freely experiment with spatial configuration. Experimental director Jerzy Grotowski, founder of the Polish Laboratory Theatre, contended that the essence of theatre lies in the communion between actor and audience. According to Grotowski, beyond that central relationship, all other theatrical elements, including text, costume, lights, and sound effects, are superfluous. Grotowski's fascination with the primacy of the connection between performer and audience led him to experiment with spatial composition and actor/audience proxity in many of his productions. Grotowski sought to break down barriers between audience and play by making spectators co-participants in the creative event. For his 1962 production of *Kordian*, for example, audience members were incorporated into the action, becoming patients in a mental ward. A year later, in his version of Christopher Marlowe's *Doctor Faustus*, spectators were seated at long tables and treated as guests at a banquet.

The hallmarks of Environmental Theatre include experimentation with spatial composition, multiple focal, and the use of "found" spaces, such as garages and warehouses, instead of traditional theatre buildings. A pioneer of Environmental Theatre, director Richard Schechner founded the Performance Group in 1967. For his production of *Makbeth*, the audience moved through and around a series of wooden structures to reach multiple performance spaces. They entered through a narrow, maze-like passageway covered with mirrors and calligraphy and then navigated ramps, stairs, towers, trapdoors, ladders, and multilevel platforms to witness various scenes. Since several scenes often played simultaneously, the audience member's experience was partially conditioned by his/her choice of focus and locale within the space.

In 1988, avant-garde theatre company Brith Gof staged a dramatization of the epic Welsh poem "Gododdin" using only six performers. The setting, an abandoned sand-filled car factory in Cardiff, was a fitting metaphor for the city's industrial and economic depression. Littered with oil barrels and old cars, the derelict factory provided a striking modern juxtaposition to the archaic language of the historical poem.

Extension

Open Air Shakespeare

In the following activity, students will collaborate to stage a lively scene from *A Midsummer Night's Dream*. The scene will be rehearsed and presented outdoors. The organic performance space will pose specific challenges, such as distractions and noise that will require strong concentration and vocal energy. On the other hand, working in an organic space will inspire bolder and more playful performance choices.

Although the scene includes only four speaking roles, every member of the class will be an active participant in its staging. To facilitate collaboration, full class involvement, and effective use of time, two actors will share each speaking part. One actor will read the lines from offstage, eliminating the need for memorization, while his/her partner in the role will physicalize the character's actions.

Ask students to volunteer for specific tasks from the list below:

Activity

- Reader: Four readers will vocalize the roles of Lysander, Helena, Demetrius, and Hermia.

- Physical Actor: Six performers will perform the physical actions of the four young lovers, plus Oberon and Puck, who witness the argument between them.

- Director: A student, rather than the teacher, should assume this function. The director will serve as an outside eye, letting the actors know when they cannot be heard, or when their action choices are unclear.

- Environmental actors: A flexible number of performers will embody the physical setting, portraying natural elements (trees, briars, bodies of water, vines) that provide obstacles for the actors to negotiate. The environmental actors should bring a high degree of mischievous playfulness to their roles. They should directly intervene in the action, creating barriers that entangle, trip up, and frustrate the human beings as they try to navigate the enchanted landscape.

- At the conclusion of the scene, the instructor will initiate a feedback session, asking students to share their feelings about the challenges and rewards of performing in an organic setting.

Scene

LYSANDER
Stay, gentle Helena; hear my excuse,
My love, my life, my soul, fair Helena!

HELENA
O excellent!

HERMIA
Sweet, do not scorn her so.

DEMETRIUS
If she cannot entreat, I can compel.

LYSANDER
Thou canst compel no more than she entreat:
Thy threats have no more strength than her weak prayers.
Helen, I love thee, by my life, I do!
I swear by that which I will lose for thee,
To prove him false that says I love thee not.

DEMETRIUS
I say I love thee more than he can do.

LYSANDER
If thou say so, withdraw, and prove it too.

DEMETRIUS
Quick, come!

HERMIA
Lysander, whereto tends all this?

LYSANDER
Away, you Ethiope!

DEMETRIUS
No, no; he'll
Seem to break loose-take on as you would follow,
But yet come not: you are a tame man, go!

LYSANDER
Hang off, thou cat, thou burr! Vile thing, let loose,
Or I will shake thee from me like a serpent!

HERMIA
Why are you grown so rude? What change is this?
Sweet love,--

LYSANDER
Thy love! Out, tawny Tartar, out!
Out, loathed medicine! O hated potion, hence!

HERMIA
Do you not jest?

HELENA
Yes, sooth; and so do you.

LYSANDER
Demetrius, I will keep my word with thee.

DEMETRIUS
I would I had your bond, for I perceive
A weak bond holds you. I'll not trust your word.

LYSANDER
What, should I hurt her, strike her, kill her dead?
Although I hate her, I'll not harm her so.

HERMIA
What, can you do me greater harm than hate?
Hate me! Wherefore? O me! What news, my love!
Am not I Hermia? Are not you Lysander?
I am as fair now as I was erewhile.

Since night you loved me; yet since night you left me:
Why, then you left me (O, the gods forbid!)
In earnest, shall I say?

LYSANDER
Ay, by my life;
And never did desire to see thee more.
Therefore be out of hope, of question, of doubt;
Be certain, nothing truer; 'tis no jest
That I do hate thee and love Helena.

HERMIA
O me! you juggler! you canker-blossom!
You thief of love! What, have you come by night
And stolen my love's heart from him?

HELENA
Fine, i'faith!
Have you no modesty, no maiden shame,
No touch of bashfulness? What, will you tear
Impatient answers from my gentle tongue?
Fie, fie, you counterfeit, you puppet, you!

HERMIA
Puppet? Why so? Ay, that way goes the game.
Now I perceive that she hath made compare
Between our statures; she hath urged her height;
And with her personage, her tall personage,
Her height, forsooth, she hath prevail'd with him.
And are you grown so high in his esteem;
Because I am so dwarfish and so low?
How low am I, thou painted maypole? Speak!
How low am I? I am not yet so low
But that my nails can reach unto thine eyes.

HELENA
I pray you, though you mock me, gentlemen,
Let her not hurt me: I was never curst;
I have no gift at all in shrewishness;

I am a right maid for my cowardice:
Let her not strike me. You perhaps may think,
Because she is something lower than myself,
That I can match her.

HERMIA
Lower! hark, again.

HELENA
Good Hermia, do not be so bitter with me.
I evermore did love you, Hermia,
Did ever keep your counsels, never wrong'd you;
Save that, in love unto Demetrius,
I told him of your stealth unto this wood.
He follow'd you; for love I follow'd him;
But he hath chid me hence and threaten'd me
To strike me, spurn me, nay, to kill me too:
And now, so you will let me quiet go,
To Athens will I bear my folly back
And follow you no further. Let me go:
You see how simple and how fond I am.

HERMIA
Why, get you gone. Who is't that hinders you?

HELENA
A foolish heart, that I leave here behind.

HERMIA
What, with Lysander?

HELENA
With Demetrius.

LYSANDER
Be not afraid; she shall not harm thee, Helena.

DEMETRIUS
No, sir, she shall not, though you take her part.

HELENA
O, when she's angry, she is keen and shrewd!
She was a vixen when she went to school;
And though she be but little, she is fierce.

HERMIA
'Little' again! nothing but 'low' and 'little?'
Why will you suffer her to flout me thus?
Let me come to her.

LYSANDER
Get you gone, you dwarf;
You minimus, of hindering knot-grass made;
You bead, you acorn.

DEMETRIUS
You are too officious
In her behalf that scorns your services.
Let her alone: speak not of Helena;
Take not her part. For, if thou dost intend
Never so little show of love to her,
Thou shalt aby it.

LYSANDER
Now she holds me not;
Now follow, if thou darest, to try whose right,
Of thine or mine, is most in Helena.

DEMETRIUS
Follow! Nay, I'll go with thee, cheek by jowl.
Exeunt LYSANDER and DEMETRIUS

HERMIA
You, mistress, all this coil is 'long of you:
Nay, go not back.

HELENA
I will not trust you, I,
Nor longer stay in your curst company.

Your hands than mine are quicker for a fray,
My legs are longer though, to run away.
Exit

HERMIA
I am amazed, and know not what to say.
Exit

Chapter 3

The Morality of Power: *Measure for Measure*

Hence shall we see
If power changes purpose: what our seemers be.
(I, iii, 53–54)

In *Measure for Measure*, the play's major characters face wrenching ethical decisions that pit moral expediency against personal values. It is a startling play more concerned with questions than answers, in which clear-cut, black and white ethical choices give place to tones of gray. Set in a society steeped in corruption and self-interest, this powerful but disturbing play dramatizes the contradiction between private behavior and public façade as it probes the misuse of authority and the temptations of power. There are no heroes in this story; no character is entirely sympathetic or praiseworthy, and their actions, which often perplex or shock us, remind us of our own often-fragile morality.

After centuries of relative neglect on the stage, *Measure for Measure* has experienced a renaissance of interest in recent years. To students grappling with the complex ethical choices of the modern world, the play's controversial subject matter, which offended the sensibilities of some earlier viewers through its frank treatment of sexuality, seems particularly topical. In the classroom, *Measure for Measure* promises to stimulate bold discussion. It frames timely questions about the responsibilities of leadership and the ethical use of power, while it challenges students to assess their own expectations of those we place in charge of our society. Like the play's characters, whose moral standards are tested under duress, students are also asked to contemplate their own personal ethical boundaries and consider how they might balance their private wants and beliefs against the conflicting rights and needs of other people. Ultimately, *Measure for Measure* prompts students to contemplate the boundless human capacity for forgiveness in a flawed world.

Background and Context

Although *Measure for Measure* was categorized as a comedy in the First Folio, given the play's dark themes, moral ambiguity, and imperfect characters, this simplistic label makes for an uncomfortable fit. In his book *Shakespeare and his Predecessors*, critic F.S. Boas addressed this issue by inventing the term "problem play" to describe a set of Shakespearean plays, including *Measure for Measure*, *Troilus and Cressida*, and *All's Well That Ends Well*, that defy traditional genre distinctions. Writing in 1896, Boas compared Shakespeare's problem plays to the dramatic works of Henrik Ibsen and George Bernard Shaw, which at the turn of the last century addressed the pressing issues of contemporary life. Like many modern dramas, all Shakespeare's problem plays share a pessimistic, even cynical outlook that scrutinizes the unattractive underbelly of human behavior. They freely comingle elements of comedy and tragedy, and each play directs attention to a challenging moral problem that evades pat solutions. Unlike the tidy resolutions of many of his earlier works, Shakespeare's problem plays end with lingering questions. When the lights come up at the end of the performance, audience members often leave the theatre with mixed emotions—having fully experienced neither the purifying release of tragedy nor the pleasant escape of comedy, they struggle to define their own responses to these unconventional, uncomfortable, and perplexing works.

Measure for Measure was probably written in either 1603 or 1604, just before Shakespeare penned a cluster of extraordinary tragedies, including *Othello*, *King Lear*, and *Macbeth*. The most masterful of the problem plays, *Measure for Measure* presaged the beginning of the period of Shakespeare's highest artistry, which corresponded to a significant shift in the playwright's creative vision. With the problem plays, Shakespeare entered a period of brooding preoccupation with darker themes and plots, which would culminate in the devastating emotional maelstrom of his greatest tragedies. During this period, he became increasingly inclined toward depicting complex characters beset by internal contradictions and inconsistencies. The memorable cast of characters of *Measure for Measure* is drawn from the full spectrum of humanity; its characters range from the virtuous but self-righteous protagonist Isabella, a novice nun whose falls victim to sexual harassment at the hands of a predatory civil servant, to Barnardine, an unrepentant condemned murderer who refuses to attend his own execution because he has a hangover, and Lucio, the dissolute womanizer who, as punishment for his libertine lifestyle, is forced to marry a prostitute at the play's end. By the time Shakespeare wrote *Measure for Measure*, his command of structure, character, and language had attained full flower. His linguistic maturity is evidenced by the play's skillful juxtaposition of impassioned poetry with vulgar colloquialisms borrowed from the city streets. In spite of its much- debated "problems," the play represents a masterwork of accomplishment, demonstrating Shakespeare's remarkable command of his dramaturgical tools.

Chronologically, Shakespeare's problem plays and mature tragedies coincided the waning years of the Elizabethan era and the dawn of the Stuart monarchy, a time of political, social, and cultural transition. In 1603, following the death of Queen Elizabeth after almost 50 years on the throne, the English people welcomed the arrival of their new sovereign, King James I, with hopeful anticipation. Years of uncertainty about who would succeed the unmarried Queen were happily resolved by the peaceful passage of power to the Scottish monarch. During the first few years of the new king's reign, however, optimism quickly turned to uncertainty and then to disapproval, as relations between James and the court rapidly soured. A seasoned leader who had worn the Scottish crown since infancy, King James possessed deeply entrenched personal beliefs about the practice of rule. The new monarch believed in the absolute authority of kings, who were, according to James, appointed by God to lead their subjects. A highly learned man who prided himself on his scholarly pursuits, James pored over religious and academic writings to support his extremist views on statecraft

Portrait of King James I. King James I of England and VI of Scotland, 1621 (oil on canvas) by Mytens, Daniel (1590-c.1648) National Portrait Gallery, London, UK/ The Bridgeman Art Library.

and authored two treatises that outlined his staunch opinions. As England's sovereign, James's insistence on his divine right to govern and refusal to negotiate with opponents quickly caused severe strains between James and Parliament. The ensuing political conflicts, combined with James's extravagant indulgence of court favorites, brought about a swift erosion of national confidence in the new monarch.

In the early days of the reign of James I, however, Shakespeare undoubtedly shared the public's high hopes for the new administration. Most assuredly, the dramatist had a strong personal motivation to cultivate the goodwill of the new King, since upon his accession, the monarch had assumed patronage of Shakespeare's theatre company, which was promptly rechristened The King's Men. With royal patronage, Shakespeare's personal fortunes were now pinned to the new court.

In light of this precipitate rise in circumstances, the playwright's decision to write a play about a society brought to the brink of moral bankruptcy by a weak leader might seem politically perilous. However, some critics have suggested that Shakespeare actually conceived his portrait of the scholarly and merciful Duke Vincentio as an oblique compliment to the new monarch. This view is supported by similarities between some of the play's speeches and a treatise authored by James, entitled *Basilikon Doron*, in which the king set out his ideas about the science of rule.

Originally intended as an instructional manual for his son on the craft of kingship, *Basilikon Doron* was written by King James in 1599, four years before he hastened toward England after the death of the old Queen. The treatise, whose title means "Royal Gift" in Greek, was eventually published in numerous languages and became an international bestseller throughout Europe. It was particularly popular in England during the first years of King James's reign, when it was eagerly scanned for clues to the personality and leadership style of the new king. In *Basilikon Doron*, James advised his son, Prince Henry, about the responsibilities and duties that attend the throne and detailed the appropriate conduct for a God-fearing Christian leader. James took especial care to delineate between the attributes of a lawful king who was divinely appointed to his lofty position and a tyrant who wrongfully usurped authority. The former, according to James, remains humbly aware of his weighty and sacred responsibilities as God's appointee on earth. He is always scrupulous about using his absolute sovereignty in the best interest of his people, rather than for personal promotion. By comparison, the usurping tyrant exploits the resources of his exalted position for personal advantage and manipulates the legal system for his own selfish interests.

Given the enormous popular interest in the *Basilikon Doron*, scholars conjecture that Shakespeare deliberately selected the topic of *Measure for Measure*, with its focus on the ethical problems of rule and the misuse of authority, as a means of capitalizing on the wave of public fascination with the monarch, while simultaneously catering to the intellectual pursuits of his theatre company's new royal patron. *Measure for Measure* was performed before the monarch as part of the Christmas celebrations at court in 1604. Although history remains silent about the king's response to the play, we may assume that it was well received, since Shakespeare's acting troupe was repeatedly invited to perform at court throughout the rest of the winter season of 1604–05.

Module #1

The Problem of Power

The British historian Lord Acton once wrote, "All power tends to corrupt, and absolute power corrupts absolutely." In *Measure for Measure*, Shakespeare approaches the characterization of Angelo, a puritanical civil servant, as a case study in the temptations of power. Like *The Tragedy of Macbeth*, which traces the downward ethical spiral of an essentially honorable man seduced by ambition, *Measure for Measure* exposes the ascetic Angelo's moral collapse when entrusted with the reins of authority. Suddenly elevated to a position of power and control, the ironically named Angelo succumbs to the allure of personal wants at the expense of public good after a brief inner struggle with his moral scruples. His swift descent into abject selfishness and depravity can be viewed as a cautionary tale that warns against the allure of power and its negative influence on moral behavior.

In the play's opening scene, the audience learns that Vienna, the site of the dramatic action, has fallen into debauchery under the indulgent leadership of Duke Vincentio. Prostitution, street crime, gambling, and promiscuity have become rampant problems in the city. Concerned about the state of deteriorating public morality, the nominal ruler of Vienna, Duke Vincentio, creates a fictitious plan to leave the city, leaving government in the hands of his deputy Angelo, who he believes will restore order through strict adherence to the law. Curious about the impact of this sudden rise in power on the character of his pious servant, the Duke disguises himself as a friar and lingers in the city to spy on Angelo.

Basking in his new cloak of authority, Angelo's confidence in his own moral infallibility and contempt for the weaknesses of others make him a strict judge. He reinstates harsh penalties on the judicial books for moral transgressions, including sexual misconduct. Determined to eradicate Vienna's thriving sex trade, Angelo promptly shuts downs the city's bawdy houses, including the brothel of Mistress Overdone. The deputy's relentless public crackdown on private sin precipitates the play's central line of action. When a respectable young man, Claudio, impregnates his betrothed sweetheart Juliet, the swift arm of the law descends. Claudio is sentenced to death, the prescribed penalty for fornication, even though he is engaged to marry the young woman he has compromised.

Shakespeare drew his antagonist Angelo from the ranks of the professional class. During the early sixteenth century, this stratum of the social framework was undergoing subtle changes as it enjoyed increasing equality of opportunity. By the reign of James I, rigid social barriers were finally beginning to shift almost imperceptibly. Although Stuart England still retained the basic class structure inherited from the Middle Ages, education and personal abilities were finally beginning to open doors for ambitious and talented young men of lesser birth (see Stone, *The Crisis of the Aristocracy*, 1967). As a member of this new upwardly mobile social class, Angelo's prospects ride on his personal reputation. Deprived of the advantages of riches or high birth, Angelo's name is everything.

Shakespeare echoes Angelo's divided nature in his two starkly opposing renderings of Vienna's city life. The city's orderly and controlled facade, with its focus on ultra-conservative morality enforced through shame and the ever-present threat of corporal discipline, competes with the enticements of the city's pleasure zones, which offer gratification of every carnal desire. Like the city he governs, Angelo hides his darker character under the outward guise of stern morality and restraint. Because of the machinations of Duke Vincentio, who tests Angelo's character through the intoxicating influence of unexpected power, Angelo's hypocrisy is forced into the harsh light of public and self-scrutiny. His secret nature is revealed when Isabella, a novice nun who is Claudio's sister, appeals to the deputy to spare her brother's life. Consumed by obsessive desire for the chaste young woman, Angelo tries to force Isabella to have sex with him in exchange for her brother's life. When Isabella threatens to reveal his sexual blackmail, the juxtaposition between Angelo's austere public image and his hidden corruption risks public exposure. By the play's end, Angelo's steep fall from grace offers an unsparing reminder of the dangers of indulging private ambition at the expense of personal values.

Measure for Measure asks challenging philosophical questions about power and morality that remain urgently pertinent today. In the holistic classroom, *Measure for Measure* motivates thoughtful discussion about conflicts between the dictates of moral conscience and self-promotion. Through the contrasting administrative styles of Duke Vincentio and Angelo, the play dramatizes the neglect of stewardship on one hand and the misuse of privilege on the other. In the public sphere, the pursuit of self-interest remains a commonplace byproduct of authority, which offers powerful temptations to those entrusted with the means to serve the public good. The play's provocative themes prompt consideration of the appropriate uses of public and personal power and our responsibilities toward those who are deprived of a voice in society.

Extension

Physicalizing Rank, Alliance, and Social Status

In this extension, students will look at ways in which the highly codified use of gesture and movement during the Tudor/Stuart era reflected interpersonal rank. Through a series of physicalization exercises, they will explore social hierarchy in *Measure for Measure* and consider how an actor might employ physical stance, spatial distance, and gesture to convey awareness of a character's social status and attitudes toward self and others. The following exercises will require students to analyze the characters' interrelationships and render conclusions about how the gender, profession, and alliances of each member of the cast of characters affects the play's overarching power dynamic. The progressive activities will also demonstrate how power shifts dramatically in the course of the play, highlighting turning points in the plot and significant actions that upend the status quo.

In democratic societies, we are taught that all men and women are equal. Although this fundamental human truth does not, unfortunately, translate into a utopian society free from prejudice, it represents an overriding modern social philosophy in direct opposition to the views prevalent during Shakespeare's lifetime. Nowadays it is difficult to relate to the idea of immovable social positions. As children, we are taught to believe that we can improve our life situation through determination and hard work. But in the Renaissance, society still clung to belief in the divine fitness of the Great Chain of Being. Handed down from the Middle Ages, this metaphor contended that social order is ordained by God, and that rebellion against one's fixed social position is both sinful and dangerous to the stability of the whole of society. Every member of society was born into his/her position on the chain, and opportunities to climb the social ladder were severely limited.

Throughout history, social rank has always carried visual signifiers of privilege and prestige. Today, material goods serve as the major visual indicators of social status. Designer clothing, large homes, and high-end cars symbolize our economic security and personal accomplishments. While material consumption was also a significant symbol of wealth and status during Shakespeare's lifetime, the human body provided a rich nonverbal language for acknowledging and reinforcing one's position in the social hierarchy. Offering physical deference to social superiors was an engrained part of etiquette during the Renaissance era. Bows, curtsies, and other physical social rituals indicated one's consciousness and acceptance of the fitness of social rank and privilege. Encounters with persons of higher status required that hats, a universal accessory worn by men and women of all ranks of life, were removed many times per day as a sign of respect toward social betters. Even within the family circle, formalized physical interactions reflected the inequality of household members. In many aristocratic families, for example, children were expected to remain standing in the presence of their parents as an outward gesture of obedience toward the biblical injunction to honor their father and mother (for a detailed discussion of family relationships during the period, see Stone, *The Family, Sex, and Marriage*, 1983). At public affairs such as court banquets, social identity could also be tacitly conveyed through the spatial configuration of guests; persons of elevated rank were often seated at high tables that literally raised them above guests of humbler status. Thus, during the Renaissance, in myriad everyday interactions, people from all walks of life used formalized body language and spatial composition to register and validate social hierarchy.

Even today, our brains make automatic assumptions about interpersonal relationships based in part on what we see. Although we are usually unaware of the eloquence of our body language, everyone uses his/her body to silently express feelings about other people and themselves. Formalized physical rituals, such as shaking hands or bowing, carry deeper, unspoken meaning about human relationships. They also represent a reversion to man's most primitive instincts. In the wild, animals use a variety of physical cues to indicate social dominance or submission.

During hostile or competitive situations, for example, animals may increase their visual size through erect, open posture, or assume a wide stance in order to occupy as much physical space as possible, thereby intimidating their opponent. Submissiveness is usually indicated when an animal adopts a low physical stance with the tail tucked between the legs, making the body smaller and more vulnerable in appearance. In human interpersonal behaviors, body language mimics these animal instincts, providing clues to our feelings about our relative status in the world in which we live (see Bickerton, 2009 for an intriguing examination of animal communication and the evolution of human language).

In the following activity, students will combine contextual analysis and physicality as tools for exploring rank, status, and social hierarchy in *Measure for Measure*, while also considering the innate relationship between social status, self-image, and identity. These progressive exercises will require solid familiarity with the play and its characters. They can be used as an acting tool for developing characterization, or they might serve as a springboard for further research into the play's historical context by generating discussion of gender politics, family relationships, social class, and occupations during the Stuart era. The activities detailed below will encourage consensual decision-making and collaborative discussion, while internalizing and providing concrete expression of the abstract principles of social hegemony and power alliance.

The activity is divided into four parts that may be completed in a single class period or divided over a series of classes.

Activity

Part I

- To begin, students will make simple signs with the names of characters from *Measure for Measure*. Be sure to include minor characters as well as leading roles. Turn the signs face down and then ask each class member to randomly select one of the signs. If roles are left over, simply set those name cards aside.

- Once everyone has selected a role, character name signs should be either pinned to shirts or attached to strings worn around the neck. This will help classmates readily identify which role each student is personifying.

- Ask the class to line up shoulder-to-shoulder facing the instructor/facilitator.

- The facilitator will ask the group to decide which character owns the highest rank at the beginning of the play. Once a consensus has been reached, ask the person portraying that dominant role to come to the head of the line.

- Next, the facilitator will instruct participants to select a place in the line that reflects their relative rank in the social hierarchy of the play. The higher one's social rank, the closer that person's line position should be in relation to the alpha character (the character of highest rank). Since a character's status may shift significantly during the course of the play, at this point in the exercise, all students should use the beginning of the play as their point of reference; even if their character does not appear in the opening scenes, they can consider the established world of the play in Act I to determine their character's appropriate placement. For this initial line-up, participants should not consult with other students, but should base their decision solely on their individual interpretation of their character's social rank. Consider that other factors besides birth might affect hierarchical status, such as gender, alliance, wealth, age, or profession.

- After the line has formed, ask students to collectively assess the line order. Encourage anyone who feels he/she is incorrectly situated to move to a new position that more accurately reflects his/her character's rank. With rare exceptions, those participants who feel compelled to move will relocate to a position higher in the line. This reordering may stimulate some debate between students who disagree about their characters' relative ranks. If a stalemate develops, the facilitator should ask each person who wishes to change his/her position within the line to explain his or her reasoning. This sharing of ideas will likely elicit group discussion about the historical significance of specific occupations during the Stuart era and may clarify the status of minor characters whose position within the configuration is initially unclear. In case of continued debate, encourage participants to conjecture about the relative importance of gender, age, alliance, or wealth in determining social status. Allow conversation and questioning to continue until the group arrives at a consensus and everyone is satisfied that his/her position in the lineup accurately reflects their status in the world of the play. If agreement is not reached with a reasonable time frame, ask the alpha character to decide where the opposing characters should be positioned.

Part II

- Once the group has reached an initial consensus about appropriate line order, the facilitator will ask students to consider how their characters' status changes in the course of the play. Repeat the activity based on the altered social environment at the beginning of Act II. The facilitator should remind students that when the act begins, the given circumstances of the play have altered drastically, since Duke Vincentio is disguised as a lowly friar, Claudio is in prison, and Angelo's moral purge is well underway. After the group agrees on a new line order that reflects the social upheaval of the world of the play, repeat the activity a third time, using the end of the play as the point of textual reference. Participants should note which characters experience the greatest changes in the course of the play and which remain relatively stable.

Part III

- The facilitator will instruct participants to revert to their line positions at the beginning of the play and assume a prototypical physical stance that expresses their characters' rank and self-image. Think about how posture, physical openness, and center of gravity might be used to communicate feelings about self and others.

- Once a physical stance has been discovered, participants will begin to explore their character's physicality by walking around the room. Consider how pace of movement, fluidity, and eye placement might indicate perceptions of self.

- Once participants have found a physical life for their characters, they should begin to interact with other characters. As characters meet on their journey through the space, they should make eye contact and render a quick decision about their characters' relative status. If the other character is of approximately equal rank, offer a bow of moderate depth. For persons of significantly higher or lower status, adjust the bow's depth to match the recipient's status. When encountering a person of much lower rank, for example, a more elevated character might offer a simple nod, while the person of humbler rank might assume a deep bow with eyes cast toward the ground. On the other hand, when greeting the alpha character, other characters might genuflect all the way down to the floor and hold that position until the character either passes them, or gestures for them to rise.

- As students become more confident embodying their roles, the facilitator should encourage them to experiment with other physical variables. Students might play with eye contact (or lack of it), for example, to indicate hostility, fawning admiration, insolence, or a host of other unspoken feelings. Likewise, the length of time that characters hold a bow might be used to say a great deal about the relationship between characters. A quick, cursory bow could pay superficial homage, while telegraphing true underlying feelings of disrespect toward the recipient. On the other hand, an overly flowery bow or curtsy by a character such as Lucio could be used as a form of nonverbal sarcasm to express feelings of dislike or flippancy. Spatial distance provides a third variable for physical experimentation. Characters possessing high rank might be given wide physical berths in accordance with their social 'size.' Alternatively, characters might indicate threat or contempt toward another character by deliberating intruding on that person's personal space.

Part IV

■ Students should now have a strong sense of their character's self-identity and relationships within the play's environment. Based on this embodied knowledge, the facilitator will instruct the participants to create a living statue that illustrates the power structure and alliances at the beginning of the play. The actors should experiment with levels, composition, focus, and physical contact to create a group portrait that represents the respective ranks of the play's characters and their primary relationships.

Reflection

1. As you moved around the room, how did it make you feel to encounter a character of higher status? If you personified one of the characters that possesses relatively low status in the play, how did the constant need to show physical deference to those of higher rank affect your emotional state?

2. How significantly does your character's status alter during the course of the play? Identify the specific factor(s) that incite your character's alteration in status. Were there specific plot points that significantly altered your character's rank? How might identification of these turning points help an actor shape a performance?

3. When you met persons of lower status, what nonverbal techniques did you use to establish dominance? How did it make you feel to have the ability to force another person to assume a subservient posture?

4. How was spatial distance used as an indicator of intimacy, homage, or aggression? If another character intruded too closely upon your personal space, what feelings did that action induce?

Module #2

Crime and Punishment in Shakespeare's England

During the Renaissance, corporal punishment was an accepted component of the bureaucratic system of law and order. In England during the Tudor and Stuart eras, physical torture and humiliation were socially sanctioned instruments of correction and repentance. In every village, the pillory and whipping post stood as mute testaments to the cultural sanction of bodily torture and bodily shaming, which were considered necessary and effective deterrents against misbehavior. Rotting heads of executed victims affixed to posts lined London Bridge, providing a grisly reminder of the ghastly consequences of misconduct. Throughout the kingdom, public executions offered a gruesome form of free, popular entertainment, and often attracted hundreds of avid spectators drawn from across the social spectrum.

Although corporal punishment was used to penalize offenders from all social classes, convicted members of the aristocracy were usually exempted from the most ghastly public punishments and were allowed to endure their suffering in private, screened from the lurid curiosity of the gaze of strangers. Thus, in Tudor society, corporal punishment not only aimed to control private behavior, but also to reinforce social divisions through unequal application of the law.

At the beginning of *Measure for Measure*, on Angelo's orders, Claudio is paraded in chains through the streets of Venice. The new deputy's motivation for this brutal public display is three-fold: it demonstrates Angelo's newfound authority, warns the populace of the harsh penalties that can be expected for violations of the standards of the new civic order, and operates as a powerful humiliation tactic that degrades Claudio's human dignity. In Vienna, 'shame' is a potent castigator; the word appears more than a dozen times in the text and is a unifying thread between many of the play's otherwise dissimilar characters.

In the twenty-first century, corporal punishment is still an accepted instrument of judicial sanction in many societies. But when physical pain and shaming tactics are used as corrective devices, they often arouse the victim's desire for retaliation. In the following activity, students will explore their responses to a game of power and control, based on the exercises of Augusto Boal's Theatre of the Oppressed.

Extension

In the 1960s, Brazilian director Augusto Boal invented an innovative form of interactive drama he called Theatre of the Oppressed. Inspired by the problems of the impoverished common people of his native country, Boal regarded theatre as a powerful vehicle for social empowerment. Over the course of four decades working with the poor and downtrodden in

South America, he created a rich arsenal of theatre games focused primarily on the human body as an instrument of expression. His improvisational activities have since been adapted for use in settings as diverse as prisons, psychotherapy sessions, and elementary school classrooms. Boal's games are designed to stimulate dialogue and critical thinking about the world's problems, and most particularly, to evoke meaningful conversation about issues of power, oppression, and exploitation of our fellow human beings.

Most of Boal's activities are body-centered, and sidestep verbal learning pathways in favor of intuitive, embodied responses. In Boal's dramatic games, the body speaks in place of the voice. All Boal's activities are coordinated and guided by a facilitator, whom Boal called The Joker. Like a joker in a deck of cards, The Joker in Boal's theatre games serves as a neutral figure without direct stakes in the game's outcome. He/she guides and coordinates the game, but encourages the game players to make discoveries on their own and rarely directly intervenes in the participants' process. The responsibility for creation lies in the hands of the participants themselves, whom Boal called spect-actors.

The following exercise is based on a simple but illuminating game that Boal entitled Columbian Hypnosis. During this game, the players will work in pairs to explore power, control, and retaliation. Given the nature of the game, before commencing play, it is essential that all players agree to adhere to some basic ground rules:

- Be respectful and trusting of your partner. Strive to work as a collaborative, noncompetitive unit.

- Do not lead your partner into dangerous or compromising situations.

- Be mindful of the movements of other teams who are also moving about the space. Protect your partner from colliding with other participants.

- Any player may stop play and sit on the sidelines whenever they feel it is necessary.

Activity

The Game

- Students will pair up for this activity. One student will agree to be the leader of the game (the Hand) and the other will be the Follower.

- To begin the game, the leader holds his/her hand six inches from the Follower's face with the fingers in front of the partner's forehead and the palm directly in front of the chin. Throughout the activity, the Follower should strive to maintain this exact distance and positioning relative to the Hand. The Follower should imagine that he/she is hypnotized by the Hand, and follow it wherever it goes throughout the space. The Follower should undertake whatever movement or body position is necessitated by the demands of the Hand. Be prepared to crawl, jump, or assume contorted postures as the Hand dictates. The Hand should aim to move the follower freely throughout the space, without losing the connection between hand and face.

- After 10 minutes of play, change positions. Repeat the exercise, with the initial Follower now in control of his/her partner's movements.

Reflection

1. How did loss of control over your decision-making power affect you? Did you trust your partner to treat you with care, protectiveness, and respect, or were you uncomfortable relinquishing personal power?

2. How did your personal relationship with your partner affect the way in which the two of you played the game? If you and your partner have a close relationship outside the classroom, did your friendship make you more willing to trust your partner? If you were paired with someone you did not know well, how did that lack of intimacy impact your willingness to blindly follow the Hand?

3. Did you feel more comfortable in the role of leader or follower? Why?

4. Was your partner a benevolent leader? Did you feel protected by your partner or were you led into positions or situations that felt threatening or embarrassing? Did you experience feelings of resentment or anxiety? If so, how did these emotions alter the way that you responded to the commands of the hand?

5. If your partner forced you to assume uncomfortable body positions, did you retaliate when it was your turn to lead? If you retaliated, how did it make you feel to get revenge for treatment you considered demeaning or unfair?

6. Did the knowledge that you could stop the game at any time increase your willingness to follow the demands of the hand? If so, what might this suggest about the reciprocal relationship between those in power and the people they lead? In the public sphere, how do elected officials solicit our trust to ensure our cooperation with their agendas?

7. Power comes in many forms. In *Measure for Measure*, what types of power are represented and misused by various characters? What message do you think Shakespeare was trying to convey by writing a play that was so preoccupied with the questionable morality of authority figures and the unscrupulous acquisition of personal power?

8. As children, we are taught to show obedience and respect toward those in authority. Are there limitations to the dictates of duty? In Nazi Germany, for example, many citizens committed atrocities through blind obedience to orders from those of higher status. Think of a situation from your own life when you confronted a situation that required you to choose between duty to an authority figure and doing what you perceived as right. What decision did you make?

9. The title of *Measure for Measure* references a passage from the Gospel of Matthew: "With what measure you mete, it shall be measured to you again" (Matt: 7: 2–3). The quote's meaning is simple: treat others the same way that you would like to be treated. At the play's conclusion, Shakespeare suggests that Angelo has learned the value of this quote. Do you believe that he has truly reformed? Is justice administered equally in the play, or is Angelo punished less harshly than Lucio? If so, why does Shakespeare make this choice?

Module #3

The Problem of Character

Alongside its thematic ambiguity and structural irregularities, one of the crucial "problems" of *Measure for Measure* resides in its deeply flawed characters, who when faced with adversity, make less than admirable decisions. Two of the play's pivotal roles, Duke Vincentio and Isabella, frequently provoke conflicting responses from readers and audience members. These deeply complicated characters can tug audience emotions in opposite directions from moment to moment, provoking our sympathies in one scene and our aversion in the next. Both characters demonstrate questionable judgment when confronted with crucial life problems and fall prey to moral equivocation that may taint the audience's initial favorable perceptions about their moral uprightness. In production, both of these nebulous roles can be interpreted from radically different angles. The play's remarkable openness allows actors to strongly mold audience reception of Isabella and the Duke through their acting choices, while helping to unlock the characters' moral complexities. Despite almost 400 years of performance history, the roles still offer fresh interpretative possibilities.

Building a Shakespearean role requires ready access to the imagination. This talent is particularly necessary for actors performing the role of Duke Vincentio, since the text of *Measure for Measure* provides sparse clues about this elusive character. The Duke's actions, which lack clear motivation on the page, confound many actors, frequently leading to uninteresting, flat performances that alienate audiences and undercut the play's dramatic power. Shakespeare never satisfactorily explains why the Duke has neglected his duties for fourteen years, allowing Vienna to become a cesspool of vice and licentiousness, and we are left to wonder about the motivations behind the Duke's sudden decision to abandon his responsibilities and enter into an elaborate game of disguise. Actors must wrestle with the play's lack of concrete guideposts toward the part as they work to build a fully dimensional characterization. For actors approaching this challenging part, Duke Vincentio poses enigmatic questions: Is he a Solomon-like ruler, a wise albeit detached leader whose intentions are wholly benevolent, even if his methods are somewhat unorthodox? Or is he a weak-willed idler who drags down his city through inattention and indecisiveness, and then, confronted with a community-wide moral crisis, retreats into hiding, forcing an underling to clean up the damage? Discovering answers to these fundamental questions forms an essential part of the actor's journey toward successfully crafting this elusive role.

As Vienna's leader-in-absentia, the Duke devises mechanisms of clandestine control that trouble many readers. Prior to going underground, his decision to delegate authority to his untested subordinate Angelo, instead of the wise elder statesman Escalus, whose diplomacy and statecraft have been proven by years of faithful service, sets the stage for a series of murky decisions. Is Duke Vincentio merely an egocentric puppeteer who delights in meddling in the private lives of his commoners? Or are we intended to interpret Vincentio as a mysterious, all-knowing, and God-like figure who serves as a distant but kindly guardian spirit over his troubled realm?

In his assumed identity as a man of God, the Duke enjoys the transplanted trust and authority of the priest's confessional role. However, he exploits the sanctity of his disguise by using it to spy into the hidden affairs of his subjects and to dupe other characters, especially the women in the play, into revealing deeply personal secrets. He masterminds the bedtrick, a strategy of questionable ethics in which Angelo's rejected lover Marianne surreptitiously takes the place of Isabella in his bed. Perhaps most troubling, Duke Vincentio impedes Isabella's avowed plans to enter the convent by publicly offering her a surprise marriage proposal that ends the play on a bewildering note.

On stage, Duke Vincentio is an often-forgettable role whose subtleties can be lost amidst a field of more sensational characters. However, despite its vagueness, the role can also serve as the centerpiece of a successful production. In the Globe Theatre's 2004 production, Mark Rylance won critical and popular praise for uncovering the role's vulnerable humanity and comedic potential. From Shakespeare's fragmentary, undefined characterization, Rylance sculpted a fully fleshed, believable character that delighted audiences. Rather than the master manipulator of some interpretations, his Duke was a well-meaning but ineffectual blunderer, a shy man reluctantly forced into the public limelight by the demands of his position. At the beginning of the play, costumed in the elaborate ruffs and ribbons of the Jacobean court, Rylance's dandified Duke was clearly out-of-touch with the lives of his people and overwhelmed by the real-life responsibilities of his position. Rylance emphasized the Duke's uncertainty and self-doubt by stumbling and stammering through many of his lines. Here was no omnipotent master planner. Instead, this likable but slightly foolish ruler gamely improvised his plans from moment to moment, making human and humorous mistakes along the way. Disguised as Friar Ludovico, he popped out of improbable hiding places, including a laundry basket, undermining the duke's decorum and lending an affectionate dose of buffoonery to the role. Through the course of the play, Rylance's Duke underwent a progressive personal transformation, gaining increased self-confidence and greater empathy for his people as he navigated the ethical intricacies of the storyline.

Over the play's performance history, responses to Isabella, the play's protagonist, have been remarkably varied. During the Victorian era, when the play was seldom performed due to its controversial sexual content, some reviewers extolled Isabella as a model of chaste femininity. Her absolute refusal to sacrifice her virginity, even at the cost of her brother's life, drew praise from many 19th Century audiences. In the modern era, however, audience members often find Isabella's rigid chastity impossible to fathom. During her first appearance in the play, Shakespeare deliberately highlights Isabella's religious extremism. We learn that Isabella has elected to enter the Sisters of St. Clare, a cloistered religious order notorious for its strictness. This initial action immediately establishes Isabella as a woman of extremes—especially when she complains that the nunnery's strictures are too lax for her tastes. Her firm confidence in her own moral superiority mirrors Angelo's, and establishes the pair as spiritual counterpoints.

In one of the plays most troubling scenes, Isabella meets with her brother Claudio in his prison cell where he is awaiting word about a possible reprieve from his death sentence.

Paola Dionisotti as Isabella, 1978. Joe Cocks Studio Collection © Shakespeare Birthplace Trust.

When Isabella reveals Angelo's offer to barter Isabella's virginity for her brother's life, Claudio begs her to accept Angelo's perverse exchange. Isabella responds to her brother's plea with equal parts of anguish and anger. She launches a remorseless attack on his sinfulness, even suggesting that Claudio's cowardice indicates that he is not the biological child of their father. The pitiless vehemence of Isabella's rant often repels viewers who are shocked by Isabella's unflinching rejection of her brother, a man facing the terrifying prospect of his own imminent mortality. Later in the play, Isabella's willing participation in the bed trick, the Duke's plot to secretly substitute Mariana for Isabella in Angelo's bed under the cover of darkness, seems paradoxical at best, given Isabella's strong moral objections to premarital sex. Throughout the play, the character's incongruities can neutralize audience empathy, but enhance our ability to make objective, critical assessments regarding her moral decisions.

Despite Isabella's perplexities, many performers regard her as one of Shakespeare's most intriguing female roles. Like Duke Vincentio, she poses controversial questions: Is she the inviolate moral center of the play toward which the audience is expected to gravitate, or an inflexible, sexually repressed prude who cares more about her chastity than her brother's life? Certainly, Isabella is neither compliant nor easily manipulated—she reveals a stubborn insistence on the rightness of her moral position, even in the face of intense pressure by male authority figures. The role offers considerable challenges to modern actresses who must wrestle with the character's contradictions and strive to win the sympathies of a modern audience that may reject her conservative sexual mores.

As an unmarried and sexually unavailable woman in hyper-sexualized Vienna, Isabella lacks a defined place within the secular community. Her decision to enter an enclosed nunnery, one that eschews contact with the outside world, offers her a defined status within a confined community. This realization of Isabella's marginalized status provided a launching point for Paola Dionisotti's interpretation of Isabella in Barry Kyle's 1978 production for the Royal Shakespeare Company.

Kyle's decision to cast Dionisotti as Isabella was a controversial choice, since the actress, who was considerably older than the actor who played her brother Claudio, contradicted stereotypical expectations of the nubile young virgin. Garbed in a nun's traditional full black habit and wimple, Dionisotti's spinsterish Isabella projected an anachronistic visual image that made clear Isabella's hopeless displacement in Vienna's seedy, pox-riddled society. Her agonized Isabella evolved through the course of the play from a severely inhibited, even fearful woman who longed for escape from a male-centered environment in which she had no place, into a mature woman awakened to her sexuality and eager for the pleasures of romantic love. Although the production itself drew some negative reviews, Dionisotti's characterization was notable for its clarity and original treatment of the play's complex gender themes.

Extension

Character Montage

Activity

- Students will select one of the three central characters from *Measure for Measure*: Duke Vincentio, Angelo, or Isabella. They will reread the play, taking note of their character's personal storyline. As students read, they should assemble a list of descriptive words that accurately reflect their character's personal traits, relationships, and journey through the action of the play. Students should pay particular attention to the contradictions and imperfections within each character, as well as their strengths, since these paradoxical characteristics lend the roles considerable depth and humanity.

- After carefully rereading the play, students should construct a back story for their character. Consider what the text tells the reader about relationships and events before the play begins and determine where holes exist in their character's personal narrative. Instruct students to rely on their imaginations to supplement known textual facts in order to supply the characters with fully detailed background stories.

- Using their back story and the list of descriptive words as a reference, each student will prepare a photographic montage that details pivotal events in their character's story history, and that conveys their interpretation of the character's essential traits. Students should be encouraged to go beyond the literal, seeking images from a wide range of styles and historical periods that remind them of their character. The only unifying thread of the images selected should be their inspiration by the character under study.

- Once the montages have been completed, the facilitator will set up a gallery of character montages and invite students to move among the pieces, viewing them at their own pace. As students examine the montages, they should note how different students "read" the same role and consider how differing image montages might inspire actors developing the role for performance and lead to unique performance approaches.

Reflection

1. In the *Basilikon Doron*, King James distinguishes between a good king and a tyrant. Does Duke Vincentio more closely resemble King James's description of the worthy ruler or the tyrant? Does the Duke use his authority and resources in responsible ways for the benefit of others, or are his actions self-serving and exploitative?

2. Angelo is usually regarded as the villain of *Measure for Measure*. But Angelo's moral crisis only arises when he is catapulted to a position of unexpected power. Might he be seen as a victim of the Duke's machinations? Is the Duke justified in testing his servant's

character through subterfuge, or does Duke Vincentio bear moral responsibility for corrupting Angelo through the temptations he places in his path?

3. When leaders violate public trust, how should society respond? Should leaders be held to a higher code of conduct than ordinary citizens? If they violate public trust, should they be removed from their positions of authority? What actions might justify such extreme measures? Is Vincentio punished in any way for his dereliction of authority and duplicity?

Module #4

The Problem Ending

The final scene of *Measure for Measure* presents one of the play's thorniest "problems". Following a public trial staged before a crowd of onlookers, the Duke offers his hand in marriage to Isabella. For many modern spectators, this contrived happy ending is deeply troubling, since the Duke's marriage proposal seems to come out of nowhere. Prior to this scene, the play has not intimated any romantic interest or attraction between the two parties, and they share little intimacy beyond the customary spiritual bonds between novice nun and friar. In contrast, Isabella's commitment to her religious vocation has been clearly established throughout the play, leading some critics to argue that it seems unlikely that Isabella—having been forced to leave the seclusion of her cloistered order by the urgent need to intercede for her brother's life—would willingly abandon her religious aspirations for a secular wedded life. At the play's end, they argue, after the degradations Isabella has endured in the outside world, it is perhaps more probable that she is eager to finally slam the door of the nunnery behind her. But does she actually retain this choice, or has Duke Vincentio's public proposal appropriated her power to make her own decision about her future?

Modern audiences are often shocked and offended by the Duke's proposal, considering it both a crass bit of trickery and a final exploitation of Isabella's trust. Shakespeare's original viewers, however, may have had a very different response, since the Duke's sudden proposal conformed to upper class marital conventions of the day. During Shakespeare's lifetime, aristocratic marriages were arranged affairs, dictated by practical concerns, such as financial gain and family alliance, rather than romantic attraction between the parties. To the play's first audience, the Duke's offer to share his bed and board with a woman of significantly lower social status might have seemed unexpectedly generous, providing a joyful conclusion to the trials of the play's troubled protagonist, who, after all her tribulations, has attained the hand of the most eligible bachelor in the land through her sterling virtue.

It is equally possible, however, that the Duke's unexpected proposal befuddled even Shakespeare's contemporaries. This view gains support from the fact that Shakespeare gives Isabella no lines after the Duke's offer of marriage. For some readers, Isabella's uncharacteristic silence indicates her reluctance, or even revulsion, toward the Duke's proposal. For others, it merely reflects happiness beyond words. In performance, Isabella's failure to speak lends the scene an openness that must be somehow negotiated. Directors are left to decide whether Isabella accepts the Duke's proposition or rejects him. Alternatively, some productions prefer to leave the question unanswered, allowing the audience to puzzle through the play's nebulous resolution.

Audiences familiar with the play often look forward to seeing how directors will handle this theatrical dilemma, and critical responses frequently hinge on this pivotal dramatic moment. John Barton's 1970 production for the Royal Shakespeare Company was one of the first to challenge traditional interpretations of the final marriage proposal. At the end of the play, the actress playing Isabella, Estelle Koehler, was left alone on stage. She stared out into the audience, clearly stunned and confused by the Duke's proposal. Barton deliberately retained the scene's textual openness, leaving audiences to guess about the play's final outcome. Almost a quarter of a century later, one of the most radical stage interpretations came in Steven Pimlott's 1994 production, in which Isabella (Stella Gonet) first slapped the astonished Duke, then passionately kissed him, and finally burst into tears. This approach clearly encapsulated Isabella's deeply conflicted response to the Duke's offer of marriage.

Extension

Isabella's Inner Monologue

For this creative activity, students will write and stage a soliloquy that gives voice to Isabella's inner monologue in the final scene.

Activity

- To begin, as a class, reread the trial scene in Act V.

- Note the textual silences within the script—the places where Isabella might be expected to speak, but does not. What is she doing and feeling during those periods of silence?

- Discuss possible stage directions that might provide indications of Isabella's state of mind. How might movement be used to express her feelings about the Duke and his proposal? How might differing physical actions radically change our perceptions of the scene?

- After the class has discussed possible actions for Isabella, students will work individually to write a soliloquy that expresses their interpretation of Isabella's feelings at the end of the play. Note that a soliloquy is addressed directly to the audience and is often used to relay a character's conflicting emotions about a situation. It invites the audience to have intimate access into the soul of the character, uninhibited by social filters.

- Have students read or perform their monologues in small groups. After everyone has presented his/her monologue, invite anyone who feels confident enough to share his/her monologue with the whole class.

Reflection

1. If Isabella accepts the Duke's marriage proposal, she will be forced to forsake her vocation as a nun. Think about a time when you were forced to give up a cherished dream in favor of a more practical choice. How did you feel about your decision at the time? Has your attitude changed?

2. Some audiences express repugnance over Isabella's refusal to sacrifice her chastity to redeem her brother's life. How do you feel about her decision? In our personal lives, how do we balance the desire for truth to self against the needs and rights of others?

Module #5

Simultaneous Dramaturgy

In Theatre of the Oppressed, Augusto Boal's primary goals were to use theatre to promote dialogue about social problems, and to encourage interaction between performer and spectator. To achieve these goals, Boal devised a technique called simultaneous dramaturgy, in which audience members were invited to problem-solve solutions to dramatic conflicts. Simultaneous dramaturgy frees audience members from their traditional constraints as silent observers and encourages them to comment on the play's action and suggest possible resolutions. By experiencing Boal's interactive theatrical techniques, audience members become co-creators of the theatrical event, while contributing toward meaningful dialogue about nonviolent solutions to human conflict.

The process of simultaneous dramaturgy involves staging a scene that depicts an oppressive situation. The scene might, for example, center on a scenario about sexual harassment in which a powerful opponent subjects an innocent victim to intimidation and abuse. After the scene has been performed once, it is restaged. During the second performance, audience members are invited to stop the action and suggest alternative actions for the oppressed character. Audience input is then incorporated into an improvised revision of the scene; thus, the spectator's direct input shapes the outcome of the reimagined scene.

Extension

Student will perform a staged reading of the following scene from *Measure for Measure* as a vehicle for applying Boal's simultaneous dramaturgy technique. The instructor will serve as the Joker, who deliberately maintains a neutral stance, avoiding personal opinions about the scene or manipulation of the outcome and moderating the discussion that accompanies the scene.

To begin the activity, two student actors will enact a sensitive excerpt from the play with scripts in hand. Due to the mature and controversial nature of the scene, following the performance, students will likely offer strong opinions about Isabella's choices in the situation. The Joker will lead students in a discussion about what they saw, heard, and felt about the dramatic situation; then the actors will begin the scene again. During this second run-through, spectators will be encouraged to stop the action whenever they have suggestions for Isabella's character that might assist her in overcoming the oppressive situation she faces. Once the action has stopped, any student who offers an idea about how to resolve Isabella's dilemma may take over the role, and try out his/her solution through an improvised departure from the script. Other characters from the play may also be interjected into the scene to change the course of the action.

Since Theatre for the Oppressed is concerned with nonaggressive problem resolution, violent solutions should be strictly avoided. In addition, the Joker should caution students against seeking magical solutions that are unsupported by the dramatic circumstances of the play.

Activity

Scene

ISABELLLA enters.

ANGELO
How now, fair maid?

ISABELLA
I am come to know your pleasure.

ANGELO
That you might know it, would much better please me
Than to demand what 'tis. Your brother cannot live.

ISABELLA
Even so. Heaven keep your honour!

ANGELO
Yet may he live awhile; and, it may be
As long as you or I.
Yet he must die.

ISABELLA
Under your sentence?

ANGELO
Yea.

ISABELLA
When, I beseech you? That in his reprieve,
Longer or shorter, he may be so fitted
That his soul sicken not.

ANGELO
Ha! fie, these filthy vices! It were as good
To pardon him that hath from nature stolen
A man already made, as to remit
Their saucy sweetness that do coin heaven's image
In stamps that are forbid: 'tis all as easy
Falsely to take away a life true made
As to put metal in restrained means
To make a false one.

ISABELLA
'Tis set down so in heaven, but not in earth.

ANGELO
Say you so? Then I shall pose you quickly.
Which had you rather: that the most just law
Now took your brother's life; or, to redeem him,
Give up your body to such sweet uncleanness
As she that he hath stain'd?

ISABELLA
Sir, believe this,
I had rather give my body than my soul.

ANGELO
I talk not of your soul: our compell'd sins
Stand more for number than for accompt.

ISABELLA
How say you?

ANGELO
Nay, I'll not warrant that; for I can speak
Against the thing I say. Answer to this:
I, now the voice of the recorded law,
Pronounce a sentence on your brother's life.
Might there not be a charity in sin
To save this brother's life?

ISABELLA
Please you to do't,
I'll take it as a peril to my soul,
It is no sin at all, but charity.

ANGELO
Pleased you to do't at peril of your soul,
Were equal poise of sin and charity.

ISABELLA
That I do beg his life, if it be sin,
Heaven let me bear it! You granting of my suit,
If that be sin, I'll make it my morn prayer
To have it added to the faults of mine,
And nothing of your answer.

ANGELO
Nay, but hear me.
Your sense pursues not mine: either you are ignorant,
Or seem so craftily; and that's not good.

ISABELLA
Let me be ignorant, and in nothing good,
But graciously to know I am no better.

ANGELO
Thus wisdom wishes to appear most bright
When it doth tax itself; as these black masks
Proclaim an enshield beauty ten times louder
Than beauty could, display'd. But mark me;
To be received plain, I'll speak more gross:
Your brother is to die.

ISABELLA
So.

ANGELO
And his offence is so, as it appears,
Accountant to the law upon that pain.

ISABELLA
True.

ANGELO
Admit no other way to save his life,—
As I subscribe not that, nor any other,
But in the loss of question,—that you, his sister,
Finding yourself desired of such a person,
Whose credit with the judge, or own great place,
Could fetch your brother from the manacles
Of the all-building law; and that there were
No earthly mean to save him, but that either
You must lay down the treasures of your body
To this supposed, or else to let him suffer;
What would you do?

ISABELLA
As much for my poor brother as myself:
That is, were I under the terms of death,
The impression of keen whips I'ld wear as rubies,
And strip myself to death, as to a bed
That longing have been sick for, ere I'ld yield
My body up to shame.

ANGELO
Then must your brother die.

ISABELLA
And 'twere the cheaper way:
Better it were a brother died at once,
Than that a sister, by redeeming him,
Should die for ever.

ANGELO
Were not you then as cruel as the sentence
That you have slander'd so?

ISABELLA
Ignomy in ransom and free pardon

Are of two houses: lawful mercy
Is nothing kin to foul redemption.

ANGELO
You seem'd of late to make the law a tyrant;
And rather proved the sliding of your brother
A merriment than a vice.

ISABELLA
O, pardon me, my lord; it oft falls out,
To have what we would have, we speak not what we mean:
I something do excuse the thing I hate,
For his advantage that I dearly love.

ANGELO
We are all frail.

ISABELLA
Else let my brother die,
If not a feodary, but only he
Owe and succeed thy weakness.

ANGELO
Nay, women are frail too.

ISABELLA
Ay, as the glasses where they view themselves,
Which are as easy broke as they make forms.
Women! Help Heaven! Men their creation mar
In profiting by them. Nay, call us ten times frail;
For we are soft as our complexions are,
And credulous to false prints.

ANGELO
I think it well:
And from this testimony of your own sex,—
Since I suppose we are made to be no stronger
Than faults may shake our frames,—let me be bold;
I do arrest your words. Be that you are,

That is, a woman; if you be more, you're none;
If you be one, as you are well express'd
By all external warrants, show it now,
By putting on the destined livery.

ISABELLA
I have no tongue but one: gentle my lord,
Let me entreat you speak the former language.

ANGELO
Plainly conceive, I love you.

ISABELLA
My brother did love Juliet,
And you tell me that he shall die for it.

ANGELO
He shall not, Isabel, if you give me love.

ISABELLA
I know your virtue hath a licence in't,
Which seems a little fouler than it is,
To pluck on others.

ANGELO
Believe me, on mine honour,
My words express my purpose.

ISABELLA
Ha! little honour to be much believed,
And most pernicious purpose! Seeming, seeming!
I will proclaim thee, Angelo; look for't:
Sign me a present pardon for my brother,
Or with an outstretch'd throat I'll tell the world aloud
What man thou art.

ANGELO
Who will believe thee, Isabel?
My unsoil'd name, the austereness of my life,

My vouch against you, and my place i' the state,
Will so your accusation overweigh,
That you shall stifle in your own report
And smell of calumny. I have begun,
And now I give my sensual race the rein:
Fit thy consent to my sharp appetite;
Lay by all nicety and prolixious blushes,
That banish what they sue for; redeem thy brother
By yielding up thy body to my will;
Or else he must not only die the death,
But thy unkindness shall his death draw out
To lingering sufferance. Answer me to-morrow,
Or, by the affection that now guides me most,
I'll prove a tyrant to him. As for you,
Say what you can, my false o'erweighs your true.

Chapter 4

The Rhetoric of Hate: *Othello*

O, beware, my lord, of jealousy!
It is the green-eyed monster which doth mock
The meat it feeds on.
(III, iii, 165–67)

One of Shakespeare's most incisive studies of human hatred, *The Tragedy of Othello* probes the destructive core of racial prejudice. The plot revolves around Iago, a military ensign whose jealousy of his black commander, Othello, a celebrated war hero, drives him to mastermind a cruel campaign to poison the thoughts of Othello and plant suspicion against his blameless wife Desdemona, while inciting public outrage against their biracial marriage. Shakespeare brilliantly utilizes the play's malicious but smooth-talking antagonist to personify the insidious power of hate rhetoric to inflame racial tensions and motivate discriminatory behavior. Pairing a gift for deception with glib verbal artistry, Iago cloaks his duplicitous actions under the garb of friendship, exploiting his privileged position as Othello's trusted confidante to harness the forces of rumor, fear, and racial bias to deftly turn character against character and precipitate the downfall of the commander he both envies and despises.

As *Othello* brilliantly dramatizes, hate language is a corrosive but often subtle form of manipulation that can fuel atrocities against the individuals or groups it targets. It persuades listeners to perceive "otherness" as a threat, something to be feared, by demonizing cultural, religious, or racial difference, or sexual preference. Playing on the innate prejudices of other characters, Iago uses his communication skills as an instrument of control, twisting the power of words into a highly efficient weapon that motivates tragic division, and ultimately, deadly violence. Through his calculated use of language, he insinuates himself into the personal insecurities of other characters, awakening their deepest fears about loss of love, honor, and self-identify.

Just as words can inflict harm, they can also heal wounded relationships. In the holistic classroom, *Othello* offers an ideal forum for generating constructive dialogue about the essential values of tolerance, equality, and inclusion, while examining the pernicious influence of hate language. By encouraging students to question their own attitudes and hidden biases, study of the play's racial themes can promote a more tolerant classroom environment where respect for difference is not simply taught, but becomes the steppingstone for cooperative inter-group relations.

Module #1

The Face of Race in Shakespeare's England

The England Shakespeare knew was neither all white nor culturally monolithic. By the late sixteenth century, major English towns, especially London, hosted a teeming, heterogeneous, and multilingual population made up of immigrants drawn from around the globe. London's ever-expanding population of around 200,000 made it one of the largest and most diverse metropolises in the world. Like Shakespeare, himself an urban transplant who left his small provincial hometown to seek fame, wealth, and adventure in the city, many immigrants were drawn to London's cosmopolitan excitements by the prospect of greater economic opportunities. Other immigrants, like the French Huguenots, Protestant religious refugees who sought escape from persecution in their own homeland, came to England as asylum seekers; still others arrived as unfortunate victims of the slave trade.

Beginning in the 1500s, English profiteers, such as John Hawkins, launched raids against coastal African villages and captured prisoners for barter in the slave commerce. When Queen Elizabeth first learned of Hawkins's traffic in human flesh, she was shocked and revolted; but when confronted with his profit sheet, she abandoned her scruples and invested in his next slaving expedition. Loaded aboard overcrowded, unsanitary ships financed by the Crown, the unfortunate captives of the English slave traders were transported far from their homes and families, most destined for a lifetime of brutal work as forced laborers in the Spanish colonies. Eventually, some black slaves and freemen found their way to the chilly shores of the English mainland, where they tried to acclimate to an alien culture in which their skin color made them visible oddities and the frequent objects of hostility and suspicion.

Members of a racial minority regarded with equal parts distrust and wonder by their white neighbors, blacks slowly began to carve out a more conspicuous, though still marginalized, presence in London life throughout the late 1500s. Although historical records are sparse, many freed blacks in Tudor/Stuart England seem to have worked in domestic service in relative obscurity. But by the late 1590s, the population of blacks in London had swelled to a sufficient size to attract negative government attention and concern. In 1596, Queen Elizabeth issued a public letter to the Lord Mayor of London, calling for the deportation of "'blackamoors', of which kind of people there are already here too many." The queen justified her order by arguing that blacks were taking employment away from native Englishmen during a period of terrible harvests and widespread hunger and economic deprivation. Elizabeth's first letter apparently yielded less than satisfying results, since it was followed by a more strongly worded order for the expulsion of black people from London in 1601. In this order, the queen buttressed her arguments by claiming that most blacks "are infidels, having no understanding of Christ or his Gospel." Like many eloquent rhetoricians, Elizabeth justified her inflammatory comments by veiling her xenophobia under the guise of concern for her white subjects. She noted that her primary responsibility rested in the well-being of those native Englishmen who were her "liege people"—that is, people just like her. Given that the queen's comments occurred during the middle years of a decades-long naval standoff with Spain, some scholars have sought to excuse Elizabeth's racist remarks by arguing that she intended to target Moors, Muslims of Arab descents who had settled in parts of Spain and Portugal during the Middle Ages, rather than people of African origin. Whatever Elizabeth's true reasoning, the letters' discriminatory language clearly denotes that racial tensions were on the rise in England.

English Renaissance literature contains abundant references to people of color. In much drama and poetry of the period, nonwhite characters are identified as strange, often barbarous objects of mystery, fear, revulsion and even evil. According to conventional notions of beauty, during the Tudor and Stuart eras, fair skin and light hair were two of the most desirable outward emblems of attractiveness. During the Tudor and Stuart eras, many high-born women, including Queen Elizabeth, applied thick, lead-based white face paint to artificially lighten skin tone, because dark skin was considered coarse, undesirable, and even ugly. Protected by the privileges of their birth status from the rigors of outdoor labor and the resulting harsh effects of the sun of their skin, ladies prized the pure white complexions that readily identified them as members of the leisured class. The Renaissance concept of correspondence also governed tastes for pale skin tone, since outward appearance supposedly correlated to inner character. As such, a white complexion was believed to denote a clean heart, pure mind, and spotless soul. As a Renaissance literary trope, dark skin color frequently figured as a negative physical and moral quality that contrasted with the ideal of whiteness and its accompanying abstract associations— purity, chastity, intellect, pure love, and honor. In opposition to the identification of white skin and blonde hair with good character, a dark complexion was equated with spiritual darkness and moral deformity; at best, it was viewed as an undesirable and pitiable deviation from the preferred white.

As a professional entertainer, Shakespeare's theatrical enterprises likely brought him into contact with a wide cross-section of London's thriving, multicultural populace. At court, where Shakespeare and his company were frequent performers, black musicians and dancers entertained the queen and her inner circle; in the less rarified environs of the professional theatre playhouses, Shakespeare's acting company shared its somewhat shady neighborhood with numerous houses of prostitution that offered the services of women representing a smorgasbord of racial origins, like the notorious courtesan Black Luce. In increasing numbers, black attendants were also engaged in aristocratic English households, where they were viewed as a popular novelty, a distinctive status symbol for their wealthy masters.

During the early years of his career in London, some scholars believe that Shakespeare may have had an intense relationship with a woman of color whom he immortalized in many of his sonnets. In Sonnet 127, the first in a sequence of sonnets addressed to a "Dark Lady," for whom the poet's feelings of love are intermingled with guilt, shame, and compulsive lust, Shakespeare plays upon the idea "blackness" as a counterbalance to "fairness," the traditional signifier of beauty and virtue. In keeping with literary conventions, in the poem, dark skin tone is posited as an outward symbol of inner darkness, a visible, external moral stain. In the Dark Lady sonnets, the poet expresses his deep internal torment over his obsession for the woman; his intense attraction for her combats with his feelings of sinfulness and self-disgust. Metaphorically, the Lady's dark skin denotes uncleanness and hidden vice; her color is a corrupt variation of white, at odds with traditional chivalric expectations of idealized, untouchable feminine beauty.

Sonnet 127

In the old age black was not counted fair,
Or if it were, it bore not Beauty's name;
But now is black Beauty's successive heir,
And Beauty slandered with a bastard shame.
For since each hand hath put on Nature's power,
Fairing the foul with Art's false borrowed face,
Sweet Beauty hath no name, no holy bower,
But is profaned, if not lives in disgrace.
Therefore my mistress' eyes are raven black,
Her eyes so suited, and they mourners seem
At such who, not born fair, no beauty lack,
Sland'ring creation with a false esteem:
Yet so they mourn becoming of their woe,
That every tongue says beauty should look so.

Despite the racial discomfort expressed in the Dark Lady sonnets, in comparison to literary norms of the era, Shakespeare's depiction of black characters is exceptionally varied and complex. The dramatist wrote several plays in which important characters are explicitly identified as black: Aaron, the unscrupulous lover of Queen Tamora in *Titus Andronicus*, The Prince of Morocco in *The Merchant of Venice*, and the title role in *Othello, the Moor of Venice*. Several other plays in the canon also feature roles that might be "read" as black: the Queen of Egypt in *Antony and Cleopatra*, or Caliban, the son of Sycorax of Algiers in *The Tempest*, for example. For *Othello*, Shakespeare may have based his leading character on a real-life role model, the exotic and glamorous Moorish ambassador Abd el-Ouahed ben Messaoud, who paid an extended visit to Queen Elizabeth's court in 1600 (For a detailed discussion of this event, see Harris 2000). Painted in a contemporary portrait garbed in full Arab robes, turban, and scimitar, the glamorous diplomat captured the public interest for several months as he sought to negotiate an anti-Spanish alliance between England and Morocco.

Portrait of Abd el-Ouahed ben Messaoud ben Mohammed Anoun, 1600. The University of Birmingham Research and Cultural Collections: copyright of the University of Birmingham.

At the time of the play's composition, around 1603, Shakespeare was lodging with a French family of "tire makers," or wigmakers, the Mountjoys, who lived in the Cripplegate parish of London (Nicholl 2007). Shakespeare's landlords and many of their neighbors were Huguenots, and part of a flourishing expatriate community made up of skilled French craftsmen who streamed into London fleeing decades of religious turmoil in their native country. Surrounded by the daily habits and conversation of his immigrant landlords, Shakespeare must have received a swift immersion into an alien language and culture. Confronted by the swelling ethnic populace of London as he traveled on his daily excursions around his adopted city, it is perhaps unsurprising that Shakespeare's creative imagination turned to issues of diversity and cultural difference.

Extension

Confronting Hidden Bias

In *Othello*, the skin color of the title character immediately sets him apart as an outsider. Despite his cultivation and personal dignity, his respected status as a war hero and staunch defender of Venice, and his conversion to Christianity, Othello's identity as a racial "other" establishes an unbridgeable distance between himself and mainstream Venetian society. When he elopes with Desdemona, Othello unleashes repressed cultural fears about interracial marriage that strip away the polite pretense of racial tolerance and reveal the true depths of racial hatred in Venice.

The issues of prejudice and racial stereotyping that confront Othello and his new wife are, of course, still current today. Modern social psychologists contend that, no matter how highly evolved and tolerant we believe ourselves to be, no one perceives race with complete neutrality. Instead, experts explain that our subconscious negative response to "otherness" is often carefully buried beneath layers of conditioned social correctness; as such, our rejection of racial difference may be deeply hidden from conscious awareness, even from ourselves. Sociologists believe that bias and stereotyping exist as relics of primitive human survival tactics. Like early man, whose survival depended on his ability to quickly differentiate friend from foe, we retain the cognitive ability to categorize others based on external characteristics. This capacity to perceive and process human difference allows us to mentally group other people into members of our "clan" versus outsiders. Individualities between those we perceive as somehow "different" from ourselves is consequently subsumed under simplistic generalities. We are usually unaware of this almost instantaneous cognitive process, but it lays the groundwork for prejudicial behavior toward others.

In today's society, most people espouse belief in egalitarianism; yet despite this avowed belief, all human beings retain unconscious biases. Heightening awareness of our hidden biases and stereotypes can help to counteract their destructive potency and prompt us to work to actively oppose them. Through the following activity, students will examine their own reflex responses to skin color. Their responses will serve as the foundation for a writing exercise that illuminates the theme of racism in *Othello*.

In order to assess unconscious biases, psychological researchers developed the Implicit Association Project. The project's aim is to design tests that measure unfiltered psychological responses to human differences, including race, religion, gender, sexual orientation, physical size, and ethnicity. Implicit Association Tests (IATs) measure test-takers' instinctive reactions to visual and language-centered stimuli that focus on these differences. While the ongoing project has confirmed that prejudice, both intentional and unintentional, remains a pervasive influence in modern culture, researchers assert that its influence can be modified through heightened awareness and deliberate efforts to modify behavior. For individual test-takers, results can provide insights into their own tendencies toward discrimination and prejudice, fostering positive efforts to change ingrained patterns of behavior.

Activity

- Students will visit the Implicit Bias project website: https://implicit.harvard.edu/implicit/demo/selectatest.html and click on the link for the Skin Tone demonstration test. Each student will complete the test and review their test results.

- Following the test, students will journal about their results. The journaling activity should provide students a private opportunity to honestly record their thoughts, without sharing them with other members of the class. Ask students to begin this contemplative activity by reflecting on the following questions:

  o What did the results of the Implicit Association Test reveal about your hidden biases?

  o How did you feel about your test results? Were your results in the range you expected? Or were you surprised by your results?

  o Do you believe that your results were accurate or inaccurate? If you believe they were inaccurate, how do you feel the test methodology could be improved to provide more accurate results?

- After students have had time to journal about their individual Implicit Association results, ask them to select one of the following prompts for an extended journal entry.

  o Select a character from Act One, scene 1. How do you think he would score on the test? Would he be surprised by his test results, or is he already aware of the degree of his prejudice? How would other characters respond if they knew your character's real feelings about race and gender? Would it change their perceptions of your character and affect their interactions?

  o In performance, Desdemona is often portrayed as a very gentle and obedient victim of circumstances, the idealized "feminine" heroine. However, her actions in the play suggest that she is a more spirited and independent woman in possession of a strong dose of self-will; after all, she dares to rebel against family and society in order to run away with the man she loves. Why is Desdemona more tolerant of Othello's difference than her peers? What personal qualities does she possess that might contribute to her tolerance, despite familial opposition to Othello's race? To what degree does social conditioning influence the ways in which we perceive race?

  o Iago uses Othello's race as a powerful instrument of propaganda, spreading fear and hatred through his deceptive use of language. Is Iago's hatred toward his commander centered exclusively on Othello's race? Or are there other reasons for his antipathy? What are they? How might this decision shape an actor's journey toward developing the role for performance?

Module #2

The Power of Words

The poet and novelist Rudyard Kipling once wrote, "Words are, of course, the most powerful drug used by mankind." In *Othello's* racially charged plot, Iago employs inflammatory racial rhetoric to vent personal jealousy, incite community tensions, and instigate interpersonal conflict. Iago's adroit use of racial slurs, innuendoes, half-suggestions, and blatant mistruths to awaken other characters' repressed biases and insecurities highlights the formidable power of words. Through his linguistic arsenal, Iago annihilates lives without raising a hand. Like a malevolent puppeteer, he creeps unseen behind the scenes, manipulating his gullible accomplices into enacting his revenge against Othello. Throughout the plot, he is able to maintain the outward pretense that he is Othello's most loyal friend and comrade-in-arms, while secretly destroying everything the Moor holds most dear.

In his campaign of destruction, words are Iago's weapon of choice. One distinctive feature of his oral dexterity is the ability to employ starkly contrasting choices of language in private versus public settings. This duality of expression is revealed only to the audience; we enact the role of Iago's sole confidante. In his soliloquies, Iago reveals to us a mastery of language that he deliberately conceals during his interactions with other characters. When speaking directly to the audience, the plain-speaking "Honest Iago" indulges in rich, image-laden verse that makes clear his intelligence and sophistication. In contrast, his dialogue with other characters is conveyed in straightforward, unembellished prose, which lends his public voice a guileless informality that invites trust and confidences. Depending on the situation and the recipient of his speech, Iago is able to expertly adapt his use to language to suit his objectives. This duplicity of speech mirrors Iago's deliberate moral deceptiveness. Like the two-faced Roman god Janus by whom Iago swears, he can assume the mask of two distinct personalities at will.

Extension

Iago and the Art of Rhetoric

In sixteenth century classrooms, rhetoric, the art of persuasive communication, was one of the central curricular components. Effective rhetorical communication, a staple of classical literature, was regarded as a defining feature of the learned Renaissance man. Rhetorical speech employs language to appeal to the listener via three major pathways: reason (Logos), feeling (Pathos), and ethics (Ethos). Virtually all methods of human argument are grounded in one of these three rhetorical avenues.

"Logos" supplies the root of the modern English word "logic." When a speaker appeals to the recipient's intellect, he/she is engaging logos as his primary persuasive tool. Logos makes use of facts, historical precedents, references to supporting experts, and carefully structured reasoning to convince listeners.

Pathos seeks to communicate through feelings by utilizing vivid imagery, impassioned vocal delivery, and recollection of emotional events to touch the heart of the listener. It seeks to compel an active response in the recipient, motivating his/her to do something specific, to right a wrong or champion a cause. Pathos is a common tool in private arguments, in editorials, opinion pieces, and the popular press. It seeks to elicit empathy in the hearer, to cause him/her to feel.

Ethos draws upon the personal credibility of the speaker to garner support for his/her viewpoint. The character and credentials of the speaker are used to establish respect and demonstrate authority, as well as to solidify identification with the audience through common interests and traits and convey trustworthiness. The audience's positive perception of the speaker is highly important in the use of ethos. Language tends to be restrained and direct, avoiding complex reasoning or highly evocative images.

In *Othello*, Iago utilizes each of the major rhetorical strategies to persuade other characters to take specific actions. The following activity will focus on identification of Iago's persuasive devices, in both a soliloquy and duet scene.

Activity

Part I

- For Part I of the following exercise, students will break into groups of three.

- Students should read aloud and discuss the Iago monologue below.

- Using different colored highlighters, mark the script to indicate where Iago uses each of the three rhetorical strategies, Ethos, Logos, or Pathos.

- As a group, decide what qualities of vocal expressiveness are appropriate to each rhetorical form. Try reading the monologue aloud again, this time dividing the lines between the three students, each of whom takes on the voice of either Ethos, Pathos, or Logos.

Soliloquy

IAGO
And what's he then that says I play the villain?
When this advice is free I give and honest,

Probal to thinking and indeed the course
To win the Moor again? For 'tis most easy
The inclining Desdemona to subdue
In any honest suit: she's framed as fruitful
As the free elements. And then for her
To win the Moor—were't to renounce his baptism,
All seals and symbols of redeemed sin,
His soul is so enfetter'd to her love,
That she may make, unmake, do what she list,
Even as her appetite shall play the god
With his weak function. How am I then a villain
To counsel Cassio to this parallel course,
Directly to his good? Divinity of hell!
When devils will the blackest sins put on,
They do suggest at first with heavenly shows,
As I do now: for whiles this honest fool
Plies Desdemona to repair his fortunes
And she for him pleads strongly to the Moor,
I'll pour this pestilence into his ear,
That she repeals him for her body's lust;
And by how much she strives to do him good,
She shall undo her credit with the Moor.
So will I turn her virtue into pitch,
And out of her own goodness make the net
That shall enmesh them all.
(II, iii, 335–62)

Part II

- To begin Part II of the exercise, the entire class will come back together as a unified group. Two students will be asked to volunteer to play the roles of Iago and Othello in the following scene. The rest of the class will assume the role of directors.

- Student directors will listen carefully to Iago's modes of speech. Each time the character shifts to a new persuasive device, directors are invited to stop the action, identify whether the character is utilizing Logos, Pathos, or Ethos, and suggest that the actor make a specific physical change that conveys Iago's new tactic. The speaker might change direction, alter the pace of his/her walk, move closer to Othello or further away, adjust the volume of his/her speech, or any other physical tactic that relays a change in strategy.

Scene

IAGO
My noble lord—

OTHELLO
What dost thou say, Iago?

IAGO
Did Michael Cassio, when you woo'd my lady,
Know of your love?

OTHELLO
He did, from first to last: why dost thou ask?

IAGO
But for a satisfaction of my thought;
No further harm.

OTHELLO
Why of thy thought, Iago?

IAGO
I did not think he had been acquainted with her.

OTHELLO
O, yes; and went between us very oft.

IAGO
Indeed!

OTHELLO
Indeed! ay, indeed: discern'st thou aught in that?
Is he not honest?

IAGO
Honest, my lord!

OTHELLO
Honest! ay, honest.

IAGO
My lord, for aught I know.

OTHELLO
What dost thou think?

IAGO
Think, my lord!

OTHELLO
Think, my lord!
By heaven, he echoes me,
As if there were some monster in his thought
Too hideous to be shown. Thou dost mean something:
I heard thee say even now, thou likedst not that,
When Cassio left my wife: what didst not like?
And when I told thee he was of my counsel
In my whole course of wooing, thou criedst 'Indeed!'
And didst contract and purse thy brow together,
As if thou then hadst shut up in thy brain
Some horrible conceit: if thou dost love me,
Show me thy thought.

IAGO
My lord, you know I love you.

OTHELLO
I think thou dost;
And, for I know thou'rt full of love and honesty,
And weigh'st thy words before thou givest them breath,
Therefore these stops of thine fright me the more:
For such things in a false disloyal knave
Are tricks of custom, but in a man that's just
They are close delations, working from the heart
That passion cannot rule.

IAGO
For Michael Cassio,
I dare be sworn I think that he is honest.

OTHELLO
I think so too.

IAGO
Men should be what they seem;
Or those that be not, would they might seem none!

OTHELLO
Certain, men should be what they seem.

IAGO
Why, then, I think Cassio's an honest man.

OTHELLO
Nay, yet there's more in this:
I prithee, speak to me as to thy thinkings,
As thou dost ruminate, and give thy worst of thoughts
The worst of words.

IAGO
Good my lord, pardon me:
Though I am bound to every act of duty,
I am not bound to that all slaves are free to.
Utter my thoughts? Why, say they are vile and false;
As where's that palace whereinto foul things
Sometimes intrude not? who has a breast so pure,
But some uncleanly apprehensions
Keep leets and law-days and in session sit
With meditations lawful?

OTHELLO
Thou dost conspire against thy friend, Iago,
If thou but think'st him wrong'd and makest his ear
A stranger to thy thoughts.

IAGO
I do beseech you—
Though I perchance am vicious in my guess,
As, I confess, it is my nature's plague

To spy into abuses, and oft my jealousy
Shapes faults that are not—that your wisdom yet,
From one that so imperfectly conceits,
Would take no notice, nor build yourself a trouble
Out of his scattering and unsure observance.
It were not for your quiet nor your good,
Nor for my manhood, honesty, or wisdom,
To let you know my thoughts.

OTHELLO
What dost thou mean?

IAGO
Good name in man and woman, dear my lord,
Is the immediate jewel of their souls:
Who steals my purse steals trash; 'tis something, nothing;
'Twas mine, 'tis his, and has been slave to thousands:
But he that filches from me my good name
Robs me of that which not enriches him
And makes me poor indeed.

OTHELLO
By heaven, I'll know thy thoughts.

IAGO
You cannot, if my heart were in your hand;
Nor shall not, whilst 'tis in my custody.

OTHELLO
Ha!

IAGO
O, beware, my lord, of jealousy;
It is the green-eyed monster which doth mock
The meat it feeds on; that cuckold lives in bliss
Who, certain of his fate, loves not his wronger;
But, O, what damned minutes tells he o'er
Who dotes, yet doubts, suspects, yet strongly loves!

OTHELLO
O misery!

IAGO
Poor and content is rich and rich enough,
But riches fineless is as poor as winter
To him that ever fears he shall be poor.
Good heaven, the souls of all my tribe defend
From jealousy!

OTHELLO
Why, why is this?
Think'st thou I'ld make a lie of jealousy,
To follow still the changes of the moon
With fresh suspicions? No; to be once in doubt
Is once to be resolved: exchange me for a goat,
When I shall turn the business of my soul
To such exsufflicate and blown surmises,
Matching thy inference. 'Tis not to make me jealous
To say my wife is fair, feeds well, loves company,
Is free of speech, sings, plays and dances well;
Where virtue is, these are more virtuous:
Nor from mine own weak merits will I draw
The smallest fear or doubt of her revolt;
For she had eyes, and chose me. No, Iago;
I'll see before I doubt; when I doubt, prove;
And on the proof, there is no more but this,—
Away at once with love or jealousy!

IAGO
I am glad of it; for now I shall have reason
To show the love and duty that I bear you
With franker spirit: therefore, as I am bound,
Receive it from me. I speak not yet of proof.
Look to your wife; observe her well with Cassio;
Wear your eye thus, not jealous nor secure:
I would not have your free and noble nature,
Out of self-bounty, be abused; look to't:
I know our country disposition well;

In Venice they do let heaven see the pranks
They dare not show their husbands; their best conscience
Is not to leave't undone, but keep't unknown.

OTHELLO
Dost thou say so?

IAGO
She did deceive her father, marrying you;
And when she seem'd to shake and fear your looks,
She loved them most.

OTHELLO
And so she did.

IAGO
Why, go to then;
She that, so young, could give out such a seeming,
To seal her father's eyes up close as oak-
He thought 'twas witchcraft—but I am much to blame;
I humbly do beseech you of your pardon
For too much loving you.

OTHELLO
I am bound to thee for ever.

IAGO
I see this hath a little dash'd your spirits.

OTHELLO
Not a jot, not a jot.

IAGO
I' faith, I fear it has.
I hope you will consider what is spoke
Comes from my love. But I do see you're moved:
I am to pray you not to strain my speech
To grosser issues nor to larger reach
Than to suspicion.

OTHELLO
I will not.

IAGO
Should you do so, my lord,
My speech should fall into such vile success
As my thoughts aim not at. Cassio's my worthy friend—
My lord, I see you're moved.

OTHELLO
No, not much moved:
I do not think but Desdemona's honest.

IAGO
Long live she so! and long live you to think so!

OTHELLO
And yet, how nature erring from itself,—

IAGO
Ay, there's the point: as—to be bold with you—
Not to affect many proposed matches
Of her own clime, complexion, and degree,
Whereto we see in all things nature tends—
Foh! one may smell in such a will most rank,
Foul disproportion thoughts unnatural.
But pardon me; I do not in position
Distinctly speak of her; though I may fear
Her will, recoiling to her better judgment,
May fall to match you with her country forms
And happily repent.

OTHELLO
Farewell, farewell:
If more thou dost perceive, let me know more;
Set on thy wife to observe: leave me, Iago:

IAGO
My lord, I take my leave.

OTHELLO
Why did I marry? This honest creature doubtless
Sees and knows more, much more, than he unfolds.

IAGO
[*Returning*] My lord, I would I might entreat
your honour
To scan this thing no further; leave it to time:
Though it be fit that Cassio have his place,
For sure, he fills it up with great ability,
Yet, if you please to hold him off awhile,
You shall by that perceive him and his means:
Note, if your lady strain his entertainment
With any strong or vehement importunity;
Much will be seen in that. In the mean time,
Let me be thought too busy in my fears—
As worthy cause I have to fear I am—
And hold her free, I do beseech your honour.

OTHELLO
Fear not my government.

IAGO
I once more take my leave.
Exit

OTHELLO
This fellow's of exceeding honesty,
And knows all qualities, with a learned spirit,
Of human dealings. If I do prove her haggard,
Though that her jesses were my dear heartstrings,
I'ld whistle her off and let her down the wind,
To pray at fortune. Haply, for I am black
And have not those soft parts of conversation
That chamberers have, or for I am declined
Into the vale of years,—yet that's not much—
She's gone. I am abused; and my relief
Must be to loathe her. O curse of marriage,
That we can call these delicate creatures ours,

And not their appetites! I had rather be a toad,
And live upon the vapour of a dungeon,
Than keep a corner in the thing I love
For others' uses. Yet, 'tis the plague of great ones;
Prerogatived are they less than the base;
'Tis destiny unshunnable, like death:
Even then this forked plague is fated to us
When we do quicken. Desdemona comes:
If she be false, O, then heaven mocks itself!
I'll not believe't.

Reflection

1. Think about the last time you had an argument. Which of the three rhetorical strategies did you rely on primarily to express your viewpoint? Was your tactic successful? In interpersonal situations, how might you express your feelings more clearly by further developing your rhetorical skills?

2. Select three television commercials that utilize Logos, Pathos, and Ethos to sell products. Why did the advertisers select their particular rhetorical tactic to persuade audiences to buy their product? Was it an effective choice? Why?

Module #3

Casting *Othello*

Over the centuries, casting practices for Shakespearean productions have clearly mirrored shifting societal attitudes about race. Because the dramatist wrote for a specific, presumably all-white company of actors, the Shakespearean canon contains few roles that distinctly demand actors of color. For many years, this scarcity of roles for black performers combined with social segregation and misguided beliefs that black actors lacked the ability or intellect to meet the demands of Shakespeare's roles to virtually exclude black actors from Shakespearean theatre. This artistic discrimination has witnessed significant reform in the past 50 years. Today, the prevalence of nontraditional casting has opened doors for nonwhite actors and encouraged audiences to see familiar roles in exciting new manifestations.

Historical Casting Practices

Shakespeare created the role of Othello for Richard Burbage, the leading tragedian of his day, for whom he also wrote such epic roles as Hamlet, King Lear, and Macbeth. Historians speculate that Burbage, who was white, probably performed the role of Othello in blackface. Today, the tradition of blackface, which involves application of dark makeup to simulate dark skin color, offends sensibilities of modern audiences educated in racial sensitivity. However, blackface was a popular theatrical convention for centuries, and remained a mainstay of vaudeville entertainment into the mid-twentieth century.

In 1833, Ira Aldridge was the first black performer to transcend racial barriers by taking on the role of *Othello*. Aldridge took over the role after Edmund Kean, a renowned white actor who was performing the part at Covent Garden Theatre in London, died during the run of the production. A seasoned Shakespearean actor who had previously played such roles as Macbeth and Richard III through the expedient of white make-up, Aldridge won critical acclaim for his dignified portrayal of the Moor; however, he also earned criticism by detractors who were shocked by the casting of a black actor against Ellen Tree, who portrayed Desdemona.

Born in New York City in 1807, Aldridge immigrated to England in search of opportunities on the stage because of insurmountable racial prejudices in the United States theatre. He quickly secured employment as an actor at the Royal Coburg Theatre, where critics dubbed him the "African Roscius." The label "Roscius," an honorific title borrowed from a classical Roman actor by that name, was traditionally bestowed upon any young performer who demonstrated extraordinary promise. Audiences flocked to see this novel sensation: a black performer who specialized in classical roles usually reserved for white men.

Over a century later, in 1930 American actor Paul Robeson became the first black performer to take on the role of Othello since Aldridge. The London production at the

Drawing of Ira Aldridge, the "African Roscius". By permission of the Folger Shakespeare Library.

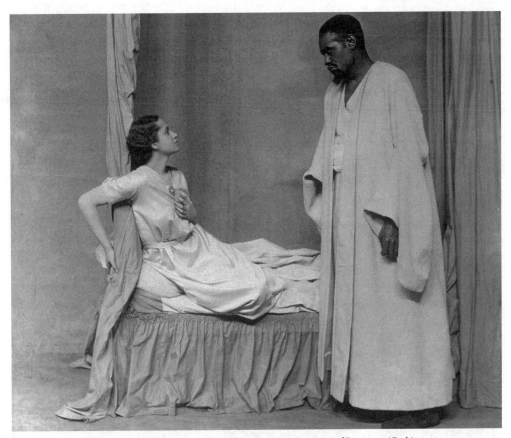

Paul Robeson and Peggy Ashcroft as Othello and Desdemona, 1930. Courtesy of Bettmann/Corbis.

Savoy Theatre was met with huge popular success. Playing the lead role opposite Peggy Ashcroft as Desdemona, Robeson received generally strong critical reviews, most of which focused on his imposing physicality and resonant voice. But one critic writing for *Sunday Times* scoffed, "There is no more reason to choose a negro to play Othello than to requisition a fat man for Falstaff."

In 1964 at the National Theatre, actor Lawrence Olivier reverted to historical tradition by performing the character of Othello in black make-up. His highly flamboyant portrayal of Othello, for which Olivier affected a vaguely West Indian dialect and lowered his vocal range an octave, spotlighted the downward spiral of an arrogant man whose life is destroyed by his pride. Othello's personification drew highly mixed reviews, with some commentators objecting strongly to Olivier's use of black face paint, which they conceived as outmoded and racist.

Lawrence Olivier as *Othello*, 1964. Houghton MS Thr 581, P922-2, Harvard Theatre Collections, Harvard University.

Actor Ben Kingsley portrayed Othello in 1986 at the Royal Shakespeare Theatre. Clad in flowing white Arab-inspired robes and headdress, Kingsley's costume provided a strong visual foil against the unrelieved black of the set's floor and walls. Although Kingsley eschewed dark make-up for the role, the cultural displacement of his distinguished and romantic Moor was highly apparent.

Dubbed the "photonegative *Othello*," Patrick Stewart played the title role in a production staged at the Shakespeare Theatre in Washington, DC in 1997. For this production, African-American actors played the roles of the white characters. This innovative approach reinvigorated dialogue about the play's treatment of race division.

Extension

Many directors claim that thoughtful and creative casting is one of the most difficult but important components to a successful production. In the following activity, students will work together in small groups to collaborate on casting a hypothetical production of *Othello*, using well-known performers of their choice. Encourage students to carefully consider not just whom they will cast, but why they are making their choices. Each group will be challenged to justify their decisions based on the following considerations:

Activity

- How might your production be cast so that a modern audience, acclimated to seeing mixed race romantic unions on television, film, and in daily life, will truly see racial difference and understand the hatreds that seethe beneath the surface of Venetian society?

- Actors frequently complain that they are locked into casting stereotypes by directors and casting agents who fail to consider them for roles outside their generalized "type". Are your casting choices based primarily on the visual appearance of the actors you select? On the types of roles that they typically play? Or on some other criteria?

- How will the style and time period of your hypothetical production influence the casting decisions that you make?

- Have you considered how effectively the overall acting ensemble will work together, or have you simply cast individual roles without consideration for their integration into a cohesive whole?

- Consider whether Othello will be the only nonwhite member of your cast. How would it change their character dynamic if both Othello and Iago were black?

- Should color-blind casting be utilized in all productions? Are there exceptions? If a white actor plays Othello, what message does that send to the audience? Should the practice of color-blind casting extend to family relationships in plays? For example, would you find it acceptable to cast an Asian Brabantio, but a Caucasian actress as his daughter Desdemona, if they are the best performers for the roles? Or would this choice confuse the audience and distract from the storyline?

Director Jude Kelly's 1997 "photo-negative" *Othello*. Patrick Stewart as Othello with Patrice Johnson as Desdemona in the Shakespeare Theatre Company's 1997 production of *Othello*. Photo by Carol Rosegg.

Module #4

Images of Cruelty

In 1938, French playwright, poet, and actor Antonin Artaud published a landmark book entitled *The Theatre and Its Double*. This groundbreaking collection of essays details Artaud's call for a radical new form of theatre that displaces the traditional primacy of the dramatic script, which Artaud referred to as "the tyranny of the text," in favor of intuitive responses and sensory saturation. In his work, Artaud rejects the centrality of logic (logos), language, and linearity that defines most Western drama. Although Artaud's revolutionary essays received little notice in the decades immediately following their publication, his theoretical writing has had a profound effect on theatrical production since the 1960s, when it became a leading influence on the experimental theatre movement and the youth subculture.

In his writings, Artaud proposed a new form of drama that he called Theatre of Cruelty. Inspired by primitive ritual and Balinese dance techniques that utilized the unspoken language of highly stylized gesture, Artaud sought to create a nontext based theatre that forced viewers to confront the implicit biases and prejudices that divide humanity, but that are usually concealed behind the outward façade of civilization. By shifting emphasis from the spoken text to the spectacle of theatre, the "poetry of senses", Artaud believed that theatre could become a place of both danger and healing. He contended that all human beings suffer from deeply entrenched, if unacknowledged hatreds that hinder our interactions with other people. His Theatre of Cruelty intended to arouse these primal emotions, to "stir up pain," thereby allowing audiences to face the anguish caused by their suppressed hatreds through the channel of a visceral theatrical experience. This intense sensory encounter, Artaud believed, would cause purgation of negative emotions and lead to heightened self-awareness for the audience members. He likened his confrontational theatre to the plague and the theatrical experience to the painful process of draining an abscess.

Theatre of Cruelty de-emphasizes text, focusing instead on codified gesture, extreme primal emotion, dance, violent images, and raw, nonverbal sound to evoke a gut-level response from the audience that circumnavigates intellectual reasoning. In his stage configurations, Artaud preferred the audience to be surrounded by the actors, who used the entire performance space to bombard the audience's senses from every direction. By destroying the traditional, safe barriers that separate actor and audience in proscenium staging, Artaud created an inescapable and disorienting spatial dynamic. Through a shocking barrage of sound, sight, and movement, Artaud believed that the audience could be liberated and cleansed of the taints of fear and hatred and discover their "doubles," their true metaphysical selves.

Extension

Despite his goal of de-emphasizing textual primary, Artaud did not entirely abandon the use of scripted language. He created scenarios that served as the creative springboard for performances. However, he wanted actors to be less invested in the literal meaning of the scripted words than in their sound quality.

The following scene from *Othello* is laced with strong racist and sexual images. This language of hate will serve as the foundation for the creation of a performance piece based on Artaud's Theatre of Cruelty techniques.

Activity

- Working in small groups of 3–4, students will compile a list of image-rich words and phrases from the scene that focus on violence, hatred, fear, sexuality, and racism.

- Once the list is assembled, try reading aloud your list of words and images. Students should feel free to rearrange the words into any random order. They should not be concerned with telling a linear story, or with replicating Shakespeare's plot. Instead, the facilitator should guide students to direct their focus to the texture, tone, and shape of the words, and the overall quality of sound. Students may experiment with whispering, shouting, devoicing, echoing, or repeating certain phrases.

- Read the list of words again. On this read-through, instruct students to only voice the consonants in each word. Are the consonant sounds hard, guttural, or sibilant? Slippery or sharp? How does the consonant order affect the sensory quality of each individual word?

- Each group will then devise a performance piece inspired by their image list. These short phrases and words may serve as the only text, or may be supplemented by invented gibberish, song, or other aural stimuli, such as rhythm and percussive elements that augment the mood and feel of the spoken word. Create a written scenario that explains the general outline of your performance piece. Use Shakespeare's language as a springboard for your own ideas.

- Using the scenario as a point of improvisation, focus on the body and voice to create a full sensory spectacle. Consider how sound effects, color, movement, rhythm, and nonverbal vocalizations might enrich your performance.

Scene

Enter RODERIGO and IAGO

RODERIGO
Tush! never tell me; I take it much unkindly
That thou, Iago, who hast had my purse
As if the strings were thine, shouldst know of this.

IAGO
'Sblood, but you will not hear me:
If ever I did dream of such a matter, Abhor me.

RODERIGO
Thou told'st me thou didst hold him in thy hate.

IAGO
Despise me, if I do not. Three great ones of the city,
In personal suit to make me his lieutenant,
Off-capp'd to him: and, by the faith of man,
I know my price, I am worth no worse a place:
But he; as loving his own pride and purposes,
Evades them, with a bombast circumstance
Horribly stuff'd with epithets of war;
And, in conclusion,
Nonsuits my mediators; for, 'Certes,' says he,
'I have already chose my officer.'
And what was he?
Forsooth, a great arithmetician,
One Michael Cassio, a Florentine,
A fellow almost damn'd in a fair wife;
That never set a squadron in the field,
Nor the division of a battle knows
More than a spinster; unless the bookish theoric,
Wherein the toged consuls can propose
As masterly as he: mere prattle, without practise,
Is all his soldiership. But he, sir, had the election:

And I, of whom his eyes had seen the proof
At Rhodes, at Cyprus and on other grounds
Christian and heathen, must be be-lee'd and calm'd
By debitor and creditor: this counter-caster,
He, in good time, must his lieutenant be,
And I—God bless the mark!—his Moorship's ancient.

RODERIGO
By heaven, I rather would have been his hangman.

IAGO
Why, there's no remedy; 'tis the curse of service,
Preferment goes by letter and affection,
And not by old gradation, where each second
Stood heir to the first. Now, sir, be judge yourself,
Whether I in any just term am affined
To love the Moor.

RODERIGO
I would not follow him then.

IAGO
O, sir, content you;
I follow him to serve my turn upon him:
We cannot all be masters, nor all masters
Cannot be truly follow'd. You shall mark
Many a duteous and knee-crooking knave,
That, doting on his own obsequious bondage,
Wears out his time, much like his master's ass,
For nought but provender, and when he's old, cashier'd:
Whip me such honest knaves. Others there are
Who, trimm'd in forms and visages of duty,
Keep yet their hearts attending on themselves,
And, throwing but shows of service on their lords,
Do well thrive by them and when they have lined their coats
Do themselves homage: these fellows have some soul;
And such a one do I profess myself. For, sir,
It is as sure as you are Roderigo,

Were I the Moor, I would not be Iago:
In following him, I follow but myself;
Heaven is my judge, not I for love and duty,
But seeming so, for my peculiar end:
For when my outward action doth demonstrate
The native act and figure of my heart
In compliment extern, 'tis not long after
But I will wear my heart upon my sleeve
For daws to peck at: I am not what I am.

RODERIGO
What a full fortune does the thicklips owe
If he can carry't thus!

IAGO
Call up her father,
Rouse him: make after him, poison his delight,
Proclaim him in the streets; incense her kinsmen,
And, though he in a fertile climate dwell,
Plague him with flies: though that his joy be joy,
Yet throw such changes of vexation on't,
As it may lose some colour.

RODERIGO
Here is her father's house; I'll call aloud.

IAGO
Do, with like timorous accent and dire yell
As when, by night and negligence, the fire
Is spied in populous cities.

RODERIGO
What, ho, Brabantio! Signior Brabantio, ho!

IAGO
Awake! what, ho, Brabantio! thieves! thieves! thieves!
Look to your house, your daughter and your bags!
Thieves! thieves!

BRABANTIO *appears above, at a window*

BRABANTIO
What is the reason of this terrible summons?
What is the matter there?

RODERIGO
Signior, is all your family within?

IAGO
Are your doors lock'd?

BRABANTIO
Why, wherefore ask you this?

IAGO
'Zounds, sir, you're robb'd; for shame, put on
your gown;
Your heart is burst, you have lost half your soul;
Even now, now, very now, an old black ram
Is topping your white ewe. Arise, arise;
Awake the snorting citizens with the bell,
Or else the devil will make a grandsire of you:
Arise, I say.

BRABANTIO
What, have you lost your wits?

RODERIGO
Most reverend signior, do you know my voice?

BRABANTIO
Not I what are you?

RODERIGO
My name is Roderigo.

BRABANTIO
The worser welcome:
I have charged thee not to haunt about my doors:
In honest plainness thou hast heard me say
My daughter is not for thee; and now, in madness,
Being full of supper and distempering draughts,
Upon malicious bravery, dost thou come
To start my quiet.

RODERIGO
Sir, sir, sir,—

BRABANTIO
But thou must needs be sure
My spirit and my place have in them power
To make this bitter to thee.

RODERIGO
Patience, good sir.

BRABANTIO
What tell'st thou me of robbing? this is Venice;
My house is not a grange.

RODERIGO
Most grave Brabantio,
In simple and pure soul I come to you.

IAGO
'Zounds, sir, you are one of those that will not
serve God, if the devil bid you. Because we come to
do you service and you think we are ruffians, you'll
have your daughter covered with a Barbary horse;
you'll have your nephews neigh to you; you'll have
coursers for cousins and gennets for germans.

BRABANTIO
What profane wretch art thou?

IAGO
I am one, sir, that comes to tell you your daughter
and the Moor are now making the beast with two backs.

BRABANTIO
Thou art a villain.

IAGO
You are—a senator.

BRABANTIO
This thou shalt answer; I know thee, Roderigo.

RODERIGO
Sir, I will answer any thing. But, I beseech you,
If't be your pleasure and most wise consent,
As partly I find it is, that your fair daughter,
At this odd-even and dull watch o' the night,
Transported, with no worse nor better guard
But with a knave of common hire, a gondolier,
To the gross clasps of a lascivious Moor—
If this be known to you and your allowance,
We then have done you bold and saucy wrongs;
But if you know not this, my manners tell me
We have your wrong rebuke. Do not believe
That, from the sense of all civility,
I thus would play and trifle with your reverence:
Your daughter, if you have not given her leave,
I say again, hath made a gross revolt;
Tying her duty, beauty, wit and fortunes
In an extravagant and wheeling stranger
Of here and every where. Straight satisfy yourself:
If she be in her chamber or your house,
Let loose on me the justice of the state
For thus deluding you.

BRABANTIO
Strike on the tinder, ho!
Give me a taper! call up all my people!
This accident is not unlike my dream:
Belief of it oppresses me already.
Light, I say! light!

Reflection

1. How did concentration on the racist and sexist language affect the scene? Did certain colors or images help you to connect to the language on a more authentic level?

2. Were you comfortable expressing words and images that are usually discouraged in modern society? Were you able to fully connect to each specific word or phrase, or did you shy away from certain images? If so, why?

3. Consider a time when you were the victim of teasing or verbal bullying. How did you handle the situation and overcome the power of words?

4. In his book, *Dreams from My Father*, Barack Obama, the son of an African man and a white woman, notes that his parent's marriage in 1960 would have been a felony offense in many states. He writes: "Miscegenation: It is a humpbacked word, ugly, portending a monstrous outcome. . . . It evokes images of another era, a distant world of horsewhips and flames, dead magnolias and crumbling porticos." What comparisons and differences exist between the marriage between Othello and Desdemona, and the senior Obamas? Have social attitudes about interracial marriage changed significantly since 1960? Or since 1603? How does race help define self-identity today?

Module #5:

The *Fabel* and *Gestus* of *Othello*

In many ways the theoretical opposite of Antonin Artaud, German director and playwright Bertolt Brecht also sought to liberate theatre from its conventional emphasis on dramatic texts. But while Artaud created a new form of theatre that used emotion and sensation as its primary dramatic tools, Brecht advocated a theatre of reason that intellectually engaged the spectator, while minimizing emotional empathy with the characters and their predicament. If Pathos ruled Artaud's Theatre of Cruelty, Logos and Ethos dominated Brecht's Epic Theatre. Brecht, a devoted Marxist, wished his theatre to provoke clear-headed debate about contemporary problems and stimulate positive social action based on the political ideas his works advanced. Brecht's performance approach was highly theatricalized and deliberately bypassed psychological realism, the dominant production mode of the day.

In the early twentieth century, Russian producer, director, actor, and teacher Constantin Stanislavsky popularized a mode of acting that has become known as the Stanislavsky system, or simply the "Method." Stanislavsky's system, which taught actors to relay "believable truth" by tapping into their own personal memories and emotions, radically influenced the process of actor training for the next century. Stanislavsky's performers were encouraged to construct an imaginary life for their character offstage, so that stage action seemed a natural continuation of the everyday life of the character.

Brecht's performance approach discounted Stanislavsky's highly personalized, popular, and realistic Method. Instead, Brecht trained his actors to deliberately abandon total immersion in their characters. Rather than fully embodying a role, the Brechtian actor "shows" or presents the role to the audience, much as the narrator of a play might stand slightly outside and removed from the immediate dramatic action. The Brechtian actors' emotional detachment from and lack of personal identification with their roles was intended to promote the audience's *V-effekt*, which is usually translated as "Alienation Effect." By maintaining a high degree of critical distance, or alienation, from the action and characters, the audience, according to Brecht, would be better able to form critical opinions about the drama's social themes.

The term "*fabel*" is used in Epic Theatre to define the play's story and its prevailing ethical attitude, or "*gestus*." The *fabel* conveys not only what occurs in the dramatic narrative, but how and why it occurs. To create a *fabel* requires the reader to interpret events, adopt a point of view, and select which predominant element of a plot to emphasize. This selective and thoughtfully considered interpretation might lead to the development of a unique and innovative directorial concept for a production.

The following excerpt from Brecht's "A Short Organum for the Theatre" demonstrates a possible directorial approach to *Hamlet*. In this example, Brecht shows how interpretation overlays literal action to create *fabel*:

It is an age of warriors. Hamlet's father, king of Denmark, slew the king of Norway in a successful war of spoliation. While the latter's son Fortinbras is arming for a fresh war the Danish king is likewise slain: by his own brother. The slain king's brother, now themselves kings, avert war by arranging that the Norwegian troops will cross Danish soil to launch a predatory war against Poland. But at this point the young Hamlet is summoned by his warrior father's ghost to avenge the crime committed against him.

After at first being reluctant to answer one bloody deed by another, and even preparing to go into exile, he meets young Fortinbras at the coast as he is marching with his troops to Poland. Overcome by this warrior-like example, he turns back and in a piece of barbaric butchery slaughters his uncle, his mother, and himself, leaving Denmark to the Norwegian. These events show the young man, already somewhat stout, making the most ineffective use of the Reason which he has picked up at the university of Wittenberg. In the feudal business to which he returns it simply hampers him. Faced with irrational practices, his reason is utterly impractical. He falls victim to the discrepancy between such reasoning and such action.

Brecht presents this *fabel* as only one of many possible readings of *Hamlet*, one that might inspire a production focused on the play's martial themes and casual savagery. The *fabel* clearly details a prevailing attitude that might strongly influence the production team's approach to setting, costume, sound, audience outreach, and performance style.

Extension

At the Berliner Ensemble, Brecht encouraged designers to create artistic renderings of various scenes that depicted possible stage compositions, the actors' physical stance and gesture, and the overall mood, idea, or tone of the scene. These drawings frequently evolved into storyboards that served as inspiration for Brecht's stage direction and the actors' development of character. *Gestus* refers to this prevailing ethical perspective, as well as a performance technique designed to capture the dominant physical attitude of a character. For the actor, *gestus* represents the embodied essence of a single, defining aspect of the role. Since the Berliner Ensemble performed for many international audiences that spoke no German, this detailed focus on physical specificity allowed the company to tell its story unhindered by language barriers.

Activity

- Students will work in pairs to script a *fabel* for *Othello*. The *fabel* should be in narrative form, and clearly focus on the racial tensions within the play. The *fabel* should articulate a distinct point of view that will clearly defines the world of the play. What sort of society is this? What values does it hold most dear?

- Using their devised *fabel*, the pair will construct a storyboard based on the play. The storyboard should not only tell the literal story, but should convey the *fabel* that has been created by the students.

Reflection

1. Using your *fabel* as a starting point, what would your production of *Othello* look like onstage? What colors, lines, and shapes might dominate your set? What theatrical style would it employ?

2. How might your *fabel* invite thoughtful dialogue about the play? Consider how you would moderate a decision based on the ideas raised by your *fabel*.

3. The Greek dramatic theorist Aristotle suggested the theatre takes audiences on a vicarious emotional journey. Through empathizing with the protagonist and his/her feelings, the audience is able to experience strong emotions within the safe setting of the theatre. Once they leave the theatre, audience members are then able to return to their everyday lives in a state of emotional moderation. In stark contrast, Brecht's Epic Theatre aimed to cultivate the audience's intellectual distance from dramatic events and characters. It consciously de-emphasized audience empathy through alienation techniques, such as disrupting the narrative with songs and discouraging actors from immersing in their characters. Which of these devices is more common in modern entertainment, such as television and film? Why? What does its approach say about contrasting views of the nature of theatre and its function in modern society?

Chapter 5

Art, Science, and Mysticism: *The Tempest*

O, wonder!
How many goodly creatures are there here!
How beauteous mankind is! O brave new world,
That has such people in't!
(V, I, 182–84)

Written around 1610–11, when Shakespeare was on the brink of retirement from the professional theatre, *The Tempest* was probably the dramatist's final play written as a sole author. Shakespeare's fanciful valediction to his stage career constitutes his most holistic play, representing the consummate synthesis of his prodigious artistic craftsmanship and intellectual gifts. *The Tempest's* plotting is sometimes opaque and often luminous, as the three-fold storyline weaves together many of the thematic threads considered at length in the preceding chapters: man's longing for lost paradise and need for a place of spiritual retreat; the ethical temptations of power and rule; discrimination against and mastery of the socially marginalized "other." In the holistic classroom, study of *The Tempest* unifies the polarities of art and science and stimulates students to redraw preconceived boundaries of learning and knowledge.

The story unfolds on a remote tropical island, where the magician Prospero, exiled Duke of Milan, has lived with his daughter Miranda for 12 years, following his usurpation by his brother, Antonio. The fairytale island setting is darkened by the ever-present shadow of past familial betrayal and anticipation of future revenge. Scholars usually place the play in the tradition of romance, a literary genre distinguished by its themes of magic and the supernatural, and plots that involve man-made or natural disasters, and tribulations based on separation and reconciliation, coincidence and miracles, loss and death.

The Tempest represents a wondrous structural hybrid—it is part elaborate masque, part tragicomedy, part social allegory. In the play, Shakespeare's storytelling techniques turn on juxtaposition between nature and civilization, empirical science and art, magic and reality. For this enigmatic piece of theatre, Shakespeare summons the full arsenal of stage spectacle. Music, dancing, and special effects combine to make this one of Shakespeare's most metatheatrical works. Yet, beneath its fantasy and fireworks lies a masterwork of lyrical abstraction that ponders universal questions about the boundaries of human learning and our thirst for self-knowledge. The play offers the ideal theatrical vehicle for study in the holistic classroom, since it draws on both analytical and subjective quests for knowledge to plumb the nature of human existence.

Module #1

Science, Magic and the Occult in Shakespeare's England

During the Tudor and Stuart eras, belief in the supernatural was virtually universal among all social classes. Alongside popular faith in folklore and magical healing, which was very widespread among the common people, in intellectual circles, learned doctors, scientists, philosophers, and theologians turned to the "mysterious" arts in search of answers about the realm of the unknown. Throughout the early modern period, the academic study of mathematics, theology, medicine, and astronomy became increasingly enmeshed with the pursuit of mystical arts, such as astrology and alchemy, and the lines between the disciplines grew increasingly indistinct. Nevertheless, firm distinctions remained between "dark" magic, which was regarded as an instrument of the Devil, an unnatural lure used by demonic powers to tempt and pollute men's souls, and "natural" magic, which was attributed to mysterious but scientific principles of God's natural world.

Historians speculate that Shakespeare may have modeled the character of Prospero after John Dee, a noted cartographer, mathematician, Hermetic philosopher, and geographer who served as court astrologer and scientific adviser to Queen Elizabeth. A highly respected intellectual and scholar who owned the largest collection of books in England (his personal library inventory numbered in the thousands), Dee attracted the professional trust and personal admiration of the monarch, herself a serious and devoted academic. Besides his extensive collection of books, Dee also maintained a private laboratory where he conducted experiments in alchemy and other occult art forms. Widely regarded as one of the greatest minds of his day, Dee's passionate fascination with the supernatural made him equally admired and notorious throughout Europe. Throughout his career, Dee worked industriously to ameliorate distinctions between traditional scholarship and magical study and eliminate academic biases against the occult. As a well-known and respected scientific scholar, Dee helped legitimize supernatural studies by carefully adhering to academic methodologies traditionally associated with math and science in his occult experiments. Precision, clinical observation, and rigorous collection and analysis of data became hallmarks of his experimentation in alchemy, stargazing, crystal reading, and other mystical arts. By transferring established scientific techniques to his pursuit of supernatural knowledge, Dee hoped to unlock the secrets of the universe and gain widespread acceptance for "natural" magic.

As Dee grew increasingly immersed in his study of the occult arts, he became a familiar figure on the European court circuit. He traveled relentlessly from court to court, constantly touting his imminent alchemical discoveries. Unfortunately, his passionate interest in advancing the mystical arts was marred by his inability to achieve quantifiable results. Following a series of failed, highly public alchemical experiments, Dee's reputation as a scientific genius and magus began to suffer. Amidst whispers of charlatanry, Dee's personal fortune rapidly declined after James of Scotland assumed the English throne.

In England, with the accession of James I in 1603, interest in magic and witchcraft gained even greater topical interest. James, who was a self-professed expert on theology and the supernatural, took a keen but disapproving interest in the occult. He personally penned a scholarly book on witchcraft, and claimed to have survived an assassination plot involving efforts to conjure a storm when he was aboard ship. However, unlike his predecessor Elizabeth, James took a dim view of Dee's obsession with the supernatural, which he regarded as dangerous and sinful. The new monarch's fear and suspicion of the occult eventually contributed to Dee's downfall, which when it arrived, was swift and disastrous. Accusations of witchcraft hounded Dee throughout the last years of his life, and he died in near poverty and obscurity in 1608.

Dr. Simon Forman offers another historical candidate who may have influenced Shakespeare's conception of his character Prospero. Dismissed by some of his contemporaries as a notorious quack, Forman was a fashionable, but untrained physician-astrologer whose clients represented a sweeping cross-section of London's urban society. His carefully documented casebooks, along with his personal diary, reveal intimate details about Forman's consultations with thousands of patients. His list of clients included Marie Mountjoy, Shakespeare's French landlady, as well as Emilia Lanier, the wife of a court musician and a speculative candidate for Shakespeare's Dark Lady. Forman's services ranged from the diagnosis and treatment of physical disorders, to more arcane services, such as astrological readings, weather predictions, and help locating lost items. He was perhaps most sought-after for his advice to the lovelorn and his sale of love poisons. It was also rumored that Forman was willing to dispense more lethal potions for a price. Following his death, Forman figured prominently in an infamous murder trial involving the 1613 poisoning of Sir Thomas Overbury by his wife and an accomplice. During the sensational trial, prosecutors claimed that Forman had supplied effigies and potions to the accused in order to render Overbury impotent and ultimately bring about his death.

In *The Tempest*, Shakespeare counterbalances two distinct kinds of magic: the "masculine" exploration of metaphysics and "white" magic, which was legitimized by serious academic study, versus the feminine exploitation of "dark" magic, a source of unpredictability and potential danger that offered tantalizing entry into the realm of the forbidden. As ruler of his island exile, Prospero functions simultaneously as master-scientist—a rational experimenter who observes and manipulates human behavior—and master-magician—virtuoso of the mystical and unexplainable, who by the play's end, must confront the specter of his own fallibility and decide to relinquish his magical power in order to resume an everyday life. Like the controversial genius John Dee, the learned magus Prospero's use of "rough magic" is a natural outgrowth of his masculine intellectual studies. He justifies his controversial devotion to occult books and magical experimentation because he envisions his studies as a means of improving human nature. However, Prospero's deep absorption in supernatural investigation alienates him from ordinary men. Back in Milan, his fascination with his academic studies posed a divisive obsession, serving as a motivation for his neglect of his dukedom and his distance from his own little daughter, Miranda (the

Alchemist, doctor, and fortune-teller Simon Forman. Portrait of Dr Simon Forman (1552–1611) engraved by Godfrey (engraving) (b/w photo) by Bulfinch, John (fl.1666) (after) Private Collection/ The Bridgeman Art Library.

"miraculous" or "admired"). As a sorcerer, Prospero's primary source of power is situated in his books, which miraculously survived the journey on the leaking boat that carried Prospero and his daughter to their magical island, rather than in his relationships with other human beings. Although his robes serve as the outward signifier of his status as a magus, and his wand as the tangible instrument of his craft, Prospero's intellectualism is the tool that sets him apart from his peers. Prospero's superior learning causes him to believe that he possesses the right to function as both the judge and overseer of his fellow humans and the spirits that inhabit the island. While Prospero turns his magical powers against other characters, he does so ostensibly to right injustices and enlist repentance from wrongdoers. However, his reliance on magic's potency to control the behavior of others is not entirely benevolent. He also employs magic in his own self-interest, using it to circumvent the rights of others. When Antonio's boat comes within range of the island, for example, Prospero seizes his opportunity to inflict revenge upon those who have wronged him.

Prospero's prodigious magical arts include the power of invisibility, and the ability to control the weather, create mysterious music, and induce sleep. In production, Prospero's magical arts might become interpreted as either sinister or benign. This fundamental decision can spotlight either the play's darkness or whimsy, and profoundly influence the directorial concept.

While Prospero embodies the idea of the masculine alliance between traditional learning and beneficial magic, feminine black magic is posited in the unseen character of Sycorax, Caliban's dead mother, a powerful witch from Algiers who was banished to the island as punishment for her use of malevolent sorcery. During her exile on the enchanted island, Sycorax established a tyrannical rule, enslaving its creatures and imprisoning the spirit Ariel in a pine tree when he refused to obey her evil commands. In contrast to Prospero's intellectualism, Sycorax, who functions as the magician's feminine counterpoint, exemplifies emotionalism and harmful magic. This gender distinction serves to remind readers that most witchcraft persecutions during the period were against women, while men's interest in magic were usually permitted as a form of "scholarship." According to Renaissance science, women's bodies and minds made them especially vulnerable to the temptations of magical power. Both physically and intellectually "weaker" than their male counterparts, women also were believed to lack the moral stability to resist the allures of the Devil. The territory of "natural" magic, with its focus on intellect and culturally legitimatized study, belonged to men.

Extension

Gendered Casting

In *The Tempest*, Ariel is described as a male spirit. Originally, an adolescent boy actor in Shakespeare's company would have undertaken the part. Given prohibitions against women on the stage, all acting companies had a complement of young male actors who specialized in women's roles, and played children or supernatural beings, such as the fairies in *A*

Midsummer Night's Dream. But in modern productions of *The Tempest*, a female performer often plays the role. For the following activity, students will consider how gender typing impacts audience reception of the roles of Prospero and Ariel. By first reading a scene aloud, and then viewing excerpts from two film versions of the play, students will discover how creative gender-casting can help audiences see the play's timeless themes in illuminating new ways.

Activity

- Students will divide into male–female pairings and read the scene between Prospero and Ariel in Act I, scene ii (below).

- After the first reading, students will exchange roles, with the male actor playing Ariel, and the female actor portraying Prospero. Does the scene still work? Why or why not? Beyond minor pronoun adjustments, what textual alterations are needed to make the gender reversal more playable or believable?

- Discuss how the language and interpersonal styles of Ariel and Prospero differ. What tactics does each character use to achieve his goal? Note the relative length of Prospero's lines in contrast to Ariel's lines. What does this discrepancy in line length reveal about the characters' power relationship?

- Next, students will compare directorial interpretations of the same scene in two film adaptations *of The Tempest*. In the first version, directed by Derek Jarman in 1979, the director adopted a strongly unorthodox approach to the play. Set almost entirely at night in a lonely manor on a deserted island, the play's Baroque, punk-inspired atmosphere is enlivened by intense directorial creativity. (In one memorable scene, Elisabeth Welch sings the classic tune "Stormy Weather" to the lost mariners.) Despite the film's directorial inventiveness, however, Jarman's casting choices are relatively conventional.

- Compare Jarman's version of the same scene to Julie Taymor's 2010 film. For her film adaptation, Taymor cast actress Helen Mirren as the protagonist, whom she reinvented as Prospera, the magician-wife of the dead Duke of Milan. Ben Whishaw portrays the role of Ariel. How effective was this creative casting choice? Did the gender reversal of Taymor's version enhance your enjoyment of the film or hinder it? Why or why not?

Scene

PROSPERO
Approach, my Ariel, come.

Enter ARIEL

ARIEL
All hail, great master! grave sir, hail! I come
To answer thy best pleasure; be't to fly,
To swim, to dive into the fire, to ride
On the curl'd clouds, to thy strong bidding task
Ariel and all his quality.

PROSPERO
Hast thou, spirit,
Perform'd to point the tempest that I bade thee?

ARIEL
To every article.
I boarded the king's ship; now on the beak,
Now in the waist, the deck, in every cabin,
I flamed amazement: sometime I'ld divide,
And burn in many places; on the topmast,
The yards and bowsprit, would I flame distinctly,
Then meet and join. Jove's lightnings, the precursors
O' the dreadful thunder-claps, more momentary
And sight-outrunning were not; the fire and cracks
Of sulphurous roaring the most mighty Neptune
Seem to besiege and make his bold waves tremble,
Yea, his dread trident shake.

PROSPERO
My brave spirit!
Who was so firm, so constant, that this coil
Would not infect his reason?

ARIEL
Not a soul
But felt a fever of the mad and play'd
Some tricks of desperation. All but mariners
Plunged in the foaming brine and quit the vessel,
Then all afire with me: the king's son, Ferdinand,
With hair up-staring,—then like reeds, not hair,—
Was the first man that leap'd; cried, 'Hell is empty
And all the devils are here.'

PROSPERO
Why that's my spirit!
But was not this nigh shore?

ARIEL
Close by, my master.

PROSPERO
But are they, Ariel, safe?

ARIEL
Not a hair perish'd;
On their sustaining garments not a blemish,
But fresher than before: and, as thou badest me,
In troops I have dispersed them 'bout the isle.
The king's son have I landed by himself;
Whom I left cooling of the air with sighs
In an odd angle of the isle and sitting,
His arms in this sad knot.

PROSPERO
Of the king's ship
The mariners say how thou hast disposed
And all the rest o' the fleet.

ARIEL
Safely in harbour
Is the king's ship; in the deep nook, where once
Thou call'dst me up at midnight to fetch dew

From the still-vex'd Bermoothes, there she's hid:
The mariners all under hatches stow'd;
Who, with a charm join'd to their suffer'd labour,
I have left asleep; and for the rest o' the fleet
Which I dispersed, they all have met again
And are upon the Mediterranean flote,
Bound sadly home for Naples,
Supposing that they saw the king's ship wreck'd
And his great person perish.

PROSPERO
Ariel, thy charge
Exactly is perform'd: but there's more work.
What is the time o' the day?

ARIEL
Past the mid season.

PROSPERO
At least two glasses. The time 'twixt six and now
Must by us both be spent most preciously.

ARIEL
Is there more toil? Since thou dost give me pains,
Let me remember thee what thou hast promised,
Which is not yet perform'd me.

PROSPERO
How now? Moody?
What is't thou canst demand?

ARIEL
My liberty.

PROSPERO
Before the time be out? No more!

ARIEL
I prithee,
Remember I have done thee worthy service;

Told thee no lies, made thee no mistakings, served
Without or grudge or grumblings: thou didst promise
To bate me a full year.

PROSPERO
Dost thou forget
From what a torment I did free thee?

ARIEL
No.

PROSPERO
Thou dost, and think'st it much to tread the ooze
Of the salt deep,
To run upon the sharp wind of the north,
To do me business in the veins o' the earth
When it is baked with frost.

ARIEL
I do not, sir.

PROSPERO
Thou liest, malignant thing! Hast thou forgot
The foul witch Sycorax, who with age and envy
Was grown into a hoop? hast thou forgot her?

ARIEL
No, sir.

PROSPERO
Thou hast. Where was she born? speak; tell me.

ARIEL
Sir, in Argier.

PROSPERO
O, was she so? I must
Once in a month recount what thou hast been,
Which thou forget'st. This damn'd witch Sycorax,

For mischiefs manifold and sorceries terrible
To enter human hearing, from Argier,
Thou know'st, was banish'd: for one thing she did
They would not take her life. Is not this true?

ARIEL
Ay, sir.

PROSPERO
This blue-eyed hag was hither brought with child
And here was left by the sailors. Thou, my slave,
As thou report'st thyself, wast then her servant;
And, for thou wast a spirit too delicate
To act her earthy and abhorr'd commands,
Refusing her grand hests, she did confine thee,
By help of her more potent ministers
And in her most unmitigable rage,
Into a cloven pine; within which rift
Imprison'd thou didst painfully remain
A dozen years; within which space she died
And left thee there; where thou didst vent thy groans
As fast as mill-wheels strike. Then was this island—
Save for the son that she did litter here,
A freckled whelp hag-born—not honour'd with
A human shape.

ARIEL
Yes, Caliban her son.

PROSPERO
Dull thing, I say so; he, that Caliban
Whom now I keep in service. Thou best know'st
What torment I did find thee in; thy groans
Did make wolves howl and penetrate the breasts
Of ever angry bears: it was a torment
To lay upon the damn'd, which Sycorax
Could not again undo: it was mine art,
When I arrived and heard thee, that made gape
The pine and let thee out.

ARIEL
I thank thee, master.

PROSPERO
If thou more murmur'st, I will rend an oak
And peg thee in his knotty entrails till
Thou hast howl'd away twelve winters.

ARIEL
Pardon, master;
I will be correspondent to command
And do my spiriting gently.

PROSPERO
Do so, and after two days
I will discharge thee.

ARIEL
That's my noble master!
What shall I do? say what; what shall I do?

PROSPERO
Go make thyself like a nymph o' the sea: be subject
To no sight but thine and mine, invisible
To every eyeball else. Go take this shape
And hither come in't: go, hence with diligence!

Exit ARIEL

Reflection

1. Based on your knowledge of Tudor/Stuart society, why do you think there was such widespread belief in magical arts? What social, political, and/or religious factors might have contributed to its cultural acceptance? How does belief in the supernatural co-exist with orthodox Christianity? What Biblical support exists for belief in the occult arts?

2. If Prospero's books, robe, and wand are his magical tools, what instruments does Ariel utilize to achieve his aims? Why is this distinction significant to the play?

3. In the Shakespearean theatre, boy actors trained with the acting company and shouldered a variety of extremely challenging female roles, ranging from Juliet to Cleopatra. The demanding repertoire of women's parts suggests that Shakespeare possessed great confidence in the talents of his boy actors to produce believable performances. Today, the custom of cross-dressing continues in some "original practice" Shakespearean productions. Likewise, in Japanese Kabuki theatre, male actors play all the roles, including women's parts. Paradoxically, many Kabuki admirers believe that *onnagata* (male actors who specialize in female roles) are able to capture the essence of traditional womanhood, including feminine beauty, innocence, fidelity and elegance, more skillfully than female performers. What advantages might there be in casting a male actor in a role that specifically calls for a woman? How might this casting choice influence the overall style of the production?

4. Why are some fields of learning traditionally regarded as "masculine" or "feminine"? Do instructors in math/science courses have different expectations of male and female students than in language-oriented courses? If so, what might account for this anomaly?

Module #2

Of Cannibals and Monsters

Scholars note that, unlike most Shakespearean plays, the plot of *The Tempest* is not drawn from a single, dominant literary or historical source. However, it is likely that sensational contemporary news, including gripping accounts sent back to England about expeditions to the Americas, strongly influenced Shakespeare's choice of subject matter and method of treatment. One likely inspiration is a letter penned by William Strachey, a passenger upon the ill-fated ship *Sea Venture* that encountered a "dreadful tempest" at sea in 1609 while in route to the Virginia settlement at Jamestown. Hurricane winds blew the ship off-course during a ferocious storm before it cast safely aground in Bermuda (a conjectural setting for *The Tempest*), miraculously sparing the lives of all the ship's passengers. Once on their tropical island, however, discord broke out among the survivors; in his account, Strachey describes how the sea's passengers, like the marooned Milanese characters in *The Tempest*, descended into conspiracy and intrigue while awaiting rescue. Shakespeare seems to have borrowed many specific details about the ferocious storm in *The Tempest* directly from Strachey's fascinating eyewitness account of the hurricane that caused the wreck of *Sea Venture*, suggesting that this sensational, real-life tale of misadventure, conflict, and survival captured the imagination of Shakespeare and served as a strong reference for the play.

Evidence also intimates that Shakespeare may have been personally acquainted with Strachey, since the two men shared mutual interests and acquaintances. Strachey was a frequent theatregoer and a shareholder in the boy's acting company, Children of the Revels. As a shareholder in a rival company, Strachey likely knew Shakespeare on a professional basis via the small world of London's professional theatre. Strachey also wrote a commendatory sonnet that was published as a preface to the play, *Sejanus*, by Shakespeare's close friend Ben Jonson, offering further circumstantial evidence of a possible personal connection between the men.

In *The Tempest*, Shakespeare's most original creation is the role of Caliban, Sycorax's monstrous and deformed son. Scholars have noted that Caliban's name is a near-anagram for the word "cannibal"; this parallel supports evidence that while writing the play, Shakespeare was inspired by an essay entitled "Of Cannibals," written by the French essayist Michel de Montaigne, and published in an English translation in 1603. However, Montaigne's "noble savage" provides a stark contrast to Shakespeare's subhuman vulgarian, Caliban:

I find that there is nothing barbarous and savage in this nation, by anything that I can gather, excepting, that every one gives the title of barbarism to everything that is not in use in his own country. As, indeed, we have no other level of truth and reason than the example and idea of the opinions and customs of the place wherein we live: there is always the perfect religion, there the perfect government, there the most exact and accomplished usage of all things. They are savages at the same rate that we say fruits are wild, which nature produces of herself and by her own ordinary progress; whereas, in truth, we ought rather to call those wild whose natures we have changed by our artifice and diverted from the common order. In those, the genuine, most useful, and natural virtues and properties are vigorous and sprightly, which we have helped to degenerate in these, by accommodating them to the pleasure of our own corrupted palate. [] These nations then seem to me to be so far barbarous, as having received but very little form and fashion from art and human invention, and consequently to be not much remote from their original simplicity. The laws of nature, however, govern them still, not as yet much vitiated with any mixture of ours: but 'tis in such purity, that I am sometimes troubled we were not sooner acquainted with these people, and that they were not discovered in those better times, when there were men much more able to judge of them than we are. I am sorry that Lycurgus and Plato had no knowledge of them; for to my apprehension, what we now see in those nations, does not only surpass all the pictures with which the poets have adorned the golden age, and all their inventions in feigning a happy state of man, but, moreover, the fancy and even the wish and desire of philosophy itself; so native and so pure a simplicity, as we by experience see to be in them, could never enter into their imagination, nor could they ever believe that human society could have been maintained with so little artifice and human patchwork. I should tell Plato that it is a nation wherein there is no manner of traffic, no knowledge of letters, no science of numbers, no name of magistrate or political superiority; no use of service, riches or poverty, no contracts, no successions, no dividends, no properties, no employments, but those of leisure, no respect of kindred, but common, no clothing, no agriculture, no metal, no use of corn or wine; the very words that signify lying, treachery, dissimulation, avarice, envy, detraction, pardon, never heard of.

[] We may then call these people barbarous, in respect to the rules of reason: but not in respect to ourselves, who in all sorts of barbarity exceed them. Their wars are throughout noble and generous, and carry as much excuse and fair pretence, as that human malady is capable of; having with them no other foundation than the sole jealousy of valour. Their disputes are not for the conquest of new lands, for these they already possess are so fruitful by nature, as to supply them without labour or concern, with all things necessary, in such abundance that they have no need to enlarge their borders. And they are, moreover, happy in this, that they only covet so much as their natural necessities require: all beyond that is superfluous to them: men of the same age call one another generally brothers, those who are younger, children; and the old men are fathers to all.

In Caliban, Shakespeare created a disturbing but strangely original role. According to the Renaissance theory of correspondence, Caliban's physical disfigurement, which includes deformity and freckles, is merely the outward sign of his inner corruption, since a person's outward ugliness was believed to reflect moral depravity and essential baseness of character. On the Great Chain of Being, the subhuman Caliban is situated lower than the other characters. Not quite human, his liminal status makes him the object of the humans' fear, loathing, and bullying. Nevertheless, despite his mistreatment by the other characters, Caliban refuses to accept his inferior status. He steadfastly challenges Prospero's right to assume rule of the island, since it was previously under the control of Caliban's mother, the powerful but evil witch Sycorax. Caliban also gives free access to his uncontrolled passions and animal lust by attempting to rape Miranda, an action that irrevocably severs Prospero's goodwill, and motivates the magician to despise and mistreat his captive.

Extension

Renaissance medical theory contended that all humans contained a predominant quantity of one of the four essential organic elements, Air, Fire, Water, or Earth. Caliban is both an odd mishap of nature and the quintessential product of the Earth—heavy, cloddish, unformed, and perhaps soulless. And yet, Shakespeare gives this earth-bound creature some of the play's most glorious poetic speeches, suggesting that hidden beneath Caliban's brutish mannerisms and ugly form lies a sensitive being longing for release and acceptance.

Like the Air after which he is named, the spirit Ariel is invisible and capricious. He provides an ideal foil to the earthy Caliban, functioning as his physical and metaphorical opposite. Although Shakespeare refers to the spirit as a male character, the role embodies many qualities conventionally considered "feminine"—helpfulness, love of beauty, and aesthetic appreciation. The airy spirit is caring, nurturing, and emotional, existing most happily in the realm of imagination and creativity.

For this activity, students will design a costume that reflects the predominant natural element of one of the characters in *The Tempest*. Decide whether the character you select best personifies Fire, Earth, Water, or Air. As you design your costume, do not feel confined by any particular time period or artistic style. Instead, let your imagination take the lead. Drawing talent should not be a hindrance to this activity. The facilitator should encourage students to feel free to trace human body forms from historical drawings to provide a template for their costume designs. Consider how your character might move and select fabrics that will enhance the performer's physicality. How will the fabric reflect or absorb light? Will it be heavy or light? What do your color choices say about your interpretation of the character? Are the lines straight or curved? Masculine or feminine? Stark or heavily embellished? Is the garment structured or loose-fitting?

After the class members have completed their costume designs, each student will prepare a class presentation that details their interpretation of the character and explains the reasoning behind their design choices. When students share their designs with their peers, the facilitator should guide conversation to focus on constructive discussion, rather than negative critique. As always in the holistic classroom, the process of creation is more significant that the end product. Every interpretation of the characters should be treated as valuable, since they represent the individual responses of a diverse group of artist/scholars.

Reflection

1. Before Caliban attempted to rape his daughter, Prospero treated the malformed creature with kindness and "human care." When Prospero's party first arrived on the island, Caliban did not understand English and "babbled" in another language or in wordless sounds. Consequently, Prospero attempted to "civilize" the native by teaching him manners and taming him to follow his directions. Like the early explorers that sought to spread their ways to the native populations of the lands they conquered, Prospero wished to impose the standards of his civilization on this strange and "brutish" creature. Are Prospero's attempts to reform and civilize Caliban indicative of arrogance or "human care". Sensitivity or insensitivity?

2. Drawing upon your knowledge of the theory of correspondences, how does the social hierarchy on Prospero's island reflect a microcosm of the social order in Milan? Through what means does Prospero immediately establish himself as ruler of his displaced kingdom? How does this parallel the circumstances that led to Prospero's own exile? How does Shakespeare use the game of chess as a paradigm for the social order in *The Tempest*?

3. Caliban's parentage further confuses readings of his social identity. We are told that he is the child of the witch Sycorax and an incubus, a male demon in human form. Is Caliban human or nonhuman? If he is not human, is he more aligned with the world of spirit, like Ariel, or more closely akin to the animal kingdom, being a creature comprised of matter but no soul? Given his demonic family tree, should he be regarded as the incarnation of evil, a being to be shunned, feared, or mastered, but beyond human compassion? Or should he be pitied?

Module #3

The Age of Discovery: New Worlds/New Divisions

Shakespeare's lifetime (1564–1616) corresponded to a dynamic cultural period marked by avid fascination with the world beyond familiar European boundaries. It was an era of expanding horizons, when adventurous explorers, tempted by the allure of riches and fame, set sail for distant lands, remapping the known world, and charting fresh trade routes that increased cultural exchange and helped globalize commerce. The unprecedented spirit of exploration that characterized the late sixteenth century ushered in profound demographic changes for both Europeans nations and the indigenous peoples of the New World.

By the 1580s, Spain, England's rival superpower, had amassed vast holdings of land in the West and secured monopolies on many exotic goods. Tempted by the prospects of riches and domination, and determined to keep pace with her southern rival, England launched several ambitious sea expeditions during the last quarter of the sixteenth century. Sir Francis Drake successfully circumnavigated the world on the Golden Hind between 1577 and 1580, and Sir Walter Raleigh founded the Virginia colony of Roanake Island in 1584. But the discovery of unknown worlds and cultures not only promised novelty and adventure; it also erected new barriers between people, ushering in a spirit of colonialism that led to bloodshed and forced migration against indigenous people. Beneath its glamorous exterior, the Age of Discovery left a legacy of racial division that endures to the present day.

Extension

Voicing a Tech-Free Storm

The Tempest begins with a storm scene that must have challenged the limited special effects resources of Shakespeare's Globe Theatre. Like *King Lear*, which also features a fearsome storm, the original production probably made use of low-tech special effects created by percussion instruments and manual sound effects, such cannon balls rolled along troughs to approximate the sound of thunder. More significantly, however, the spectacle of the storm scene relied on Shakespeare's descriptive language to supply any deficits in visual stagecraft. For the following activity, students will explore line structure, punctuation, and voice as tools to dramatize the storm scene, without reliance on external technology.

Activity

- The following activity will require an open space free from furnishings.

- To start, students should read the opening storm scene (below) several times aloud to achieve strong familiarity with the content and language.

- With scripts in hand, students should stand in a tight circle.

- Once students have gained solid familiarity with the scene, they should strive to capture the high stakes, urgency, and human drama of the situation by randomly changing readers at each punctuation mark. Only one student should speak at a time, so classmates will need to be highly alert to the energy of their peers. Students should jump in whenever they feel compelled to speak, while always respecting the structure provided by the punctuation. Although it may seem difficult to keep everyone from speaking at once, once the scene gets underway, students will acquire an intuitive sense about when it is their "turn" to speak. This heightened connectedness will create a sense of ensemble that lends the storm scene excitement, reality, tension, variety, and conflict.

Scene

On a ship at sea: a tempestuous noise of thunder and lightning heard.

Enter a Master and a Boatswain

MASTER
Boatswain!

BOATSWAIN
Here, master: what cheer?

MASTER
Good, speak to the mariners: fall to't, yarely,
or we run ourselves aground: bestir, bestir.

Exit

Enter Mariners

BOATSWAIN
Heigh, my hearts! cheerly, cheerly, my hearts!
yare, yare! Take in the topsail. Tend to the
master's whistle. Blow, till thou burst thy wind,
if room enough!

Enter ALONSO and others

ALONSO
Good boatswain, have care. Where's the master?
Play the men.

BOATSWAIN
I pray now, keep below.

ANTONIO
Where is the master, boatswain?

BOATSWAIN
Do you not hear him? You mar our labour: keep your
cabins: you do assist the storm.

GONZALO
Nay, good, be patient.
Boatswain
When the sea is. Hence! What cares these roarers
for the name of king? To cabin: silence! trouble us not.

GONZALO
Good, yet remember whom thou hast aboard.

BOATSWAIN
None that I more love than myself. You are a
counsellor; if you can command these elements to
silence, and work the peace of the present, we will
not hand a rope more; use your authority: if you
cannot, give thanks you have lived so long, and make

yourself ready in your cabin for the mischance of
the hour, if it so hap. Cheerly, good hearts! Out
of our way, I say.
Exit

GONZALO
I have great comfort from this fellow: methinks he
hath no drowning mark upon him; his complexion is
perfect gallows. Stand fast, good Fate, to his
hanging: make the rope of his destiny our cable,
for our own doth little advantage. If he be not
born to be hanged, our case is miserable.
Exeunt

Re-enter Boatswain

BOATSWAIN
Down with the topmast! yare! lower, lower! Bring
her to try with main-course.
A cry within

A plague upon this howling! they are louder than
the weather or our office.

Re-enter SEBASTIAN, ANTONIO, *and* GONZALO

Yet again! what do you here? Shall we give o'er
and drown? Have you a mind to sink?

SEBASTIAN
A pox o' your throat, you bawling, blasphemous,
incharitable dog!

BOATSWAIN
Work you then.

ANTONIO
Hang, cur! hang, you whoreson, insolent noisemaker!
We are less afraid to be drowned than thou art.

GONZALO
I'll warrant him for drowning; though the ship were
no stronger than a nutshell and as leaky as an
unstanched wench.

BOATSWAIN
Lay her a-hold …, a-hold! set her two courses off to
sea again; lay her off.

Enter Mariners wet

MARINERS
All lost! to prayers, to prayers! all lost!

BOATSWAIN
What, must our mouths be cold?

GONZALO
The king and prince at prayers! let's assist them,
For our case is as theirs.

SEBASTIAN
I'm out of patience.

ANTONIO
We are merely cheated of our lives by drunkards:
This wide-chapp'd rascal—would thou mightst lie drowning
The washing of ten tides!

GONZALO
He'll be hang'd yet,
Though every drop of water swear against it
And gape at widest to glut him.
A confused noise within: 'Mercy on us!'— 'We split, we split!'—'Farewell, my wife and
children!'— 'Farewell, brother!'— 'We split, we split, we split!'

ANTONIO
Let's all sink with the king.

SEBASTIAN
Let's take leave of him.

Exeunt ANTONIO and SEBASTIAN

GONZALO
Now would I give a thousand furlongs of sea for an
acre of barren ground, long heath, brown furze, any
thing. The wills above be done! but I would fain
die a dry death.
Exeunt

Reflection

1. Notice how dividing the lines into short phrases dictated by the punctuation helps the actors capture the energy, variety, and urgency of the situation. How might an actor achieve this same quality in his/her individual line delivery?

2. Did anticipating your "turn" heighten your concentration and involvement in the scene? Did it help to create a sense of unity with your fellow performers? Did it create a competitive or collaborative climate? How might this heightened awareness of other members of the ensemble be beneficial to an actor in production?

3. How were you able to decide when it was your "turn" to speak? What nonverbal clues indicated when someone was about to take over the reading? What role did intuition and body energy play in providing nonverbal cues? Were you more conscious of the group dynamic and collective energy in the room? Why?

Module #4

The Tempest and the Science Play

In 1956, the now classic science fiction film *Forbidden Planet* attracted hoards of teenagers to movie theatres and drive-ins across America. Most were probably unaware that the campy sci-fi film they were enjoying was, in fact, an adaptation of Shakespeare's play, *The Tempest*. Updated to the year 2257, in the movie's space-age setting, Shakespeare's island utopia is transfigured into the planet Altair IV where an astronaut and his beautiful daughter have been stranded for many years following the crash of their spaceship. In the movie script, Shakespeare's Prospero and Miranda are transfigured into Dr. Edward Morbius and his daughter Altaira, their trusty robot Robby stands in for Ariel, and the destructive Monster from Id takes on the role of Caliban. Like her counterpart, Miranda in Shakespeare's play, Altaira has never seen any man except her father, and immediately becomes smitten by Commander Adams, leader of a rescue party sent to determine the fate of the missing scientist and his party.

Over the centuries, Shakespeare's play has inspired a variety of imitations and adaptations, like *Forbidden Planet*. With its themes of intellectual inquiry and experimentation, *The Tempest* might be considered an early precursor of the modern science play, especially given its focus on a eccentric academic who is devoted to the reclusive delights of his books. In common with its modern successor, the emerging science play genre, *The Tempest* features the interface of scientific inquiry and aesthetics.

As a dramatic genre, the science play has achieved significant commercial and popular success over the past quarter century. The science play genre includes a subcategory that has been coined "lab lit." Unlike traditional science fiction, which is typically set in a fantastic world of the distant future, lab lit is usually concerned with the realistic portrayal of scientists, and accurate portrayal of the laws of math and science. Technology and current ethical issues in science, such as genetic engineering and disease control, are common motifs. Lab lit and other forms of science plays explicitly represent the union of theatre and science, providing a hopeful sign of increased collaboration and discourse between the arts and sciences.

- One of the best known science plays, David Auburn's suspenseful, Pulitzer prize-winning play *Proof* centers on Catherine, the daughter of a brilliant math professor who has recently died, and the discovery of a highly significant original proof for a mathematical theorem.

- Tom Stoppard's *Arcadia* features dual plot lines set in the present day and in Regency England. The play's diverse topics, which veer from landscape design to Lord Byron to chaos theory, meld together to form a remarkable collision between art and science.

- Winner of the 2000 Tony Award for Best Play, *Copenhagen* by Michael Frayn is based on an actual historical event: a meeting during World War II between Niels Bohr, a Danish physicist of Jewish descent, and his friend Werner Heisenberg, head of the German campaign to develop an atomic bomb.

Extension

Science Play Research, Analysis, and Playwriting

- Working in three groups, students will read one of the plays listed above (*Proof, Arcadia*, or *Copenhagen*), which are readily available in libraries. Ask students to prepare a 15-minute presentation for the class that includes discussion of the play's plot, characters, style, and structure. The presentation should conclude with performance of a brief scene from the selected play. Teaching the play to their fellow students should be each group's most important goal. Therefore, encourage students to make their presentations not only informative, but also entertaining, through the use of multimedia, visuals and kinesthetic elements.

- Next, each group will write a script for a short (10-minute), modernized science play or science fiction adaptation, based on the backstory of *The Tempest*. What specific details does Shakespeare provide, and what must you infer about the relationships and events that occurred prior to the start of the play? What details must you invent? What elements of Shakespeare's play must be altered in order for it to adhere to the science play or science fiction genre?

- Perform the short play for the class.

Reflection

1. Why do you think there has been renewed interest in recent years in the depiction of scientific topics on stage?

2. Provide examples from television programs and films that focus on the interplay of art and science.

3. Research other art forms (music, visual art, dance) that effectively merge aesthetics and science. In 100 years, what new forms of art can you envision that might be derived from emerging technologies?

Module #5

The Art/Science Continuum

In the twenty-first century, art and science, for many years regarded as cognitive opposites that require radically different skills and affinities, have undergone remarkable integration. Digital artists combine aesthetics and technology to create stunningly original art; interactive media redefines the limitations of filmmaking, video, and live performance; conceptual kinetics appropriates engineering to develop mechanical devices that straddle the boundaries between function and art. In the Shakespeare classroom, *The Tempest* offers a reminder of the remarkable climate of intellectual and aesthetic openness that existed during the Renaissance, and provides fertile material for exploring the rewards that derive from nurturing connections between discrete areas of learning.

In *The Tempest*, Prospero embodies both artist and scientist. Historians speculate that Shakespeare, himself a holistic thinker unbound by the limitations of self-definition, felt a particular affinity for his final, solo-authored, protagonist. Prospero's poignant monologue denouncing his magical arts suggests a deeply personal identification between the playwright, poised on the verge of retirement, and his theatrical creation:

> Ye elves of hills, brooks, standing lakes, and groves;
> And ye that on the sands with printless foot
> Do chase the ebbing Neptune, and do fly him
> When he comes back; you demi-puppets that
> By moonshine do the green sour ringlets make,
> Whereof the ewe not bites; and you whose pastime
> Is to make midnight mushrooms, that rejoice
> To hear the solemn curfew; by whose aid,—
> Weak masters though ye be,—I have bedimm'd
> The noontide sun, call'd forth the mutinous winds,
> And 'twixt the green sea and the azur'd vault
> Set roaring war: to the dread rattling thunder
> Have I given fire, and rifted Jove's stout oak
> With his own bolt: the strong-bas'd promontory
> Have I made shake; and by the spurs pluck'd up
> The pine and cedar: graves at my command
> Have wak'd their sleepers, op'd, and let them forth
> By my so potent art. But this rough magic
> I here abjure; and, when I have requir'd
> Some heavenly music (which even now I do)
> To work mine end upon their senses that
> This airy charm is for, I'll break my staff,

Bury it certain fathoms in the earth,
And deeper than did ever plummet sound
I'll drown my book.
(V, I, 33–57)

At the play's end, in order to return to the world of civilization, Prospero must give up the love of magic and the quest for knowledge that have been his life's work and avocation. But Prospero takes with him the remembrance of a lifetime of experimentation and discovery. In contrast, conventional educational settings often urge young learners to abandon prospective pathways of learning before they have had an opportunity to explore and develop sufficient understanding about themselves to make informed decisions about their futures. Early aptitude tests and standardized test scores subtly encourage students to assume rigid self-labels too early in their academic journeys. By urging learners to adopt premature categorization as either "science/math" or "language/arts" students, counselors and teachers often discourage students from dwelling in that fascinating area of crossover, connection, and magical discovery, the corpus callosum.

Extension

Character Analysis and Brain Lateralization

As discussed in earlier chapters, brain lateralization refers to the division of cognitive functions between the left and right cerebral hemispheres. Usually, left hemispheric functions govern tasks that require linear, analytical thought, such as mathematics and science, and the ability to grasp time sequences, categorization, and goal setting. Right brain functions help us to "read" other people's nonverbal signals, such as body language, gesture, and facial expression. This side of the brain also contributes to our aesthetic appreciation and encourages playfulness. Bridging and linking the two brain hemispheres, the corpus callosum transmits communication between these complementary cerebral spheres.

Activity

- In this character analysis activity, students will use brain lateralization theory to investigate a character's personality and thought processes.

- Select any major character from *The Tempest*.

- Reread the script, noting any descriptions of the character. How do other characters describe him? How does he/she define himself/herself?

- Notice not only what the character says, but also what he/she does. The difference between stated intention and actual action is often highly revealing.

- Categorize your character's abilities, actions, and personality attributes into left or right brain functions. Note that some qualities will seem to exist in both realms simultaneously.

- Based on your character reading, is your character a left- or right-brain thinker? How might this insight influence your development of the role for performance? Would identifying your character as a left or right brainer affect your movement or change your mode of relating to other characters? If so, how?

Reflection

1. Do you consider yourself to be a predominately left or right brain thinker? How might you cultivate your ability to co-exist in both realms to your fullest potential? How comfortable are you dwelling in the realm of the corpus callosum? Which classes have helped you to explore that liminal space?

2. How might creative dramatics be used to teach math and science in the elementary classroom? In what ways might the interplay between aesthetics and scientific study prove helpful to students in other curricular areas, such as history or economics? How might continued study of Shakespeare enhance other areas of your personal growth and learning?

3. In his book, *A Whole New Mind: Moving from the Information Age to the Conceptual Age*, author Dan Pink suggests the computer era has reinforced educational preferences for left-brain qualities, like math and science skills. With the cost efficiency of mechanized labor, however, Pink predicts that, in the future, repetitive and analytical job functions will be increasingly allocated to robots and computers, or outsourced to cheap labor overseas (Pink 2005). In the business arena, he suggests that workers can increase their personal success and employability by cultivating six essential right-brain abilities qualities necessary to ensure competence and productivity in the job market:

   o Design: Pink refers to design as "business literacy," and proposes that a carefully conceived design for any product is fundamental to its success.

o   Story: Storytelling is an innate human instinct. In the business world, the ability to relate and communicate a story that binds together disconnected facts and figures is a powerful commodity.

o   Symphony: Pink defines symphony as the ability to comprehend the interconnectedness of unrelated elements and synthesize them into a related whole.

o   Empathy: According to the author, the ability to put yourself in the position of a product user and anticipate their problems and experiences is a distinctive marker of the empathic thinker.

o   Play: Pink describes play as a "marker of organizational health" that benefits creativity and leads to innovative discoveries.

o   Meaning: In the pursuit for business success, Pink notes that it is essential to remain aware of what gives meaning to your life.

Pink's book, which became an international bestseller, has developed a huge following since its publication in 2005 and made its author a much sought after motivational speaker. Why do you think his work has become so influential? How can the six right brain attributes Pink lists above be applied in the holistic Shakespeare classroom? How do these attributes correlate to the process of planning and staging a theatrical production?

Resources for Further Learning

Shakespeare is often lauded as the greatest dramatist of the English language. In the classroom, however, his status as our iconic playwright can present a double-edged sword. While his theatrical works reveal Shakespeare as an astute observer of human strengths and frailties, his plays often become dry and lifeless in the classroom. If we reverence his works as the epitome of "high culture," pedagogical approaches can tend to reinforce students' view of the plays as overly precious literary masterworks, rather than as dynamic, living, and sometimes messy works of theatre. Furthermore, when dissection of the texts becomes more important than enjoyment of the human drama they capture, students are robbed of much of the joy of studying Shakespeare. By keeping performative elements firmly at the center of the classroom experience, holistic Shakespeare ensures students' active involvement, while increasing cooperation, imagination, community building, and empathy.

Over the past quarter century, Shakespeare pedagogy has experienced dramatic progress and witnessed the contributions of numerous inspirational teachers who have revitalized the methodologies and applications of Shakespeare studies. Although not a universally recognized household name, Tina Packer is revered among Shakespearean teachers and performers. For the past three decades, she has inspired thousands of performers and teachers with her unique teaching methods. The British native is the founder and former Artistic Director of Shakespeare & Company, an acclaimed professional theatre company that Packer began in 1978 with the goal of creating a top-notch American classical theatre. Located in the scenic Berkshires, Packer's company originated as a sort of artists' commune that resided at The Mount, the historic former home of Edith Wharton. In collaboration with other renowned teachers, including voice specialist Kristin Linklater, Packer developed a distinctive teaching methodology that acknowledges the centrality of Shakespeare's language, while providing opportunities for deep personal engagement with the plays and exploration of each participant's authentic emotional truth. Working with a core teaching unit of highly trained colleagues, Packer shares her passion for Shakespeare with groups of professional actors who travel from around the globe for her intensive month-long workshops and with groups of school children who are encountering the plays for the first time. Workshops at Shakespeare and Co. incorporate clown work, Alexander movement technique, vocal training, and detailed textual analysis. Packer has also extended her work to include nontheatrical workshops with business professionals. In these workshops, she uses Shakespeare's language to teach hands-on lessons about management and leadership skills.

Richard Olivier, the son of legendary actor Lawrence Olivier, has also developed a series of Shakespeare workshops aimed at the business community. His workshops, which concentrate on what he calls Mythodrama, are directed at training inspirational leaders who possess wisdom, empathy, and respect for diverse personalities. Both Packer and Olivier exemplify the forward-reaching, progressive integration of arts and other areas of modern culture that are propelling Shakespeare into the mainstream of social relevancy and educational advancement. The successful efforts of these, and other pioneering Shakespeare teachers, prove that Shakespeare's plays continue to provide vital life lessons that can teach values that resonate far beyond the walls of the classroom.

Bibliography and Materials for Additional Study

In addition to identifying sources utilized in the preparation of this book, this section aims to point instructors toward supplemental learning materials that will enhance teaching of the content of the preceding chapters. Consultation of the materials listed below can deepen and enrich students' background information in each chapter and enhance instructor's preparation for guiding study of each unit. These varied supplemental resources can also be utilized to inform student research projects, provide extended reading opportunities, and enhance theatre-based activities in the classroom.

Preface:

Hall, Peter. (2003). *Shakespeare's Advice to the Players*. New York: TCG.

Introduction:

Books and Essays

Brockbank, Anne, McGill, Ian, and Beech, Nic. (2007). *Facilitating Reflective Learning in Higher Education*. 2nd edn. New York: Macgraw Hill.

Cook, Henry Caldwell. (1917). *The Play Way: An Essay in Educational Method*. New York: Frederick A. Stokes.

Cressy, David. (1975). *Education in Tudor and Stewart England*. New York: St. Martin's Press.

Gibson, Rex. (1998). *Teaching Shakespeare: A Handbook for Teachers*. Cambridge: Cambridge UP.

Kohn, Alfie. (2000). *The Case Against Standardized Testing: Raising the Scores, Ruining the Schools*. Portsmouth, NH: Heinemann.

(Sir Desmond Lee, trans.) (1995). *The Republic* by Plato. West Drayton: Penguin.

Linklater, Kristin. (2009). *Freeing Shakespeare's Voice: The Actor's Guide to Talking the Text*. London: Nick Hern.

Miller, J. P. (1993). *The Holistic Curriculum*. Toronto: OISE Press.

———. (1993). *The Holistic Teacher*. Toronto: OISE Press.

Moffett, James. (1994). *The Universal Schoolhouse: Spiritual Awakening Through Education*. San Francisco: Jossey-Bass.

Orme, Nicholas. (1989). *Education and Society in Medieval and Renaissance England*. London: Hambledon Press.

Pask, Gordon, and Scott, B. C. E. (1972). "Learning Strategies and Individual Competence." *International Journal of Man-Medicine Studies*, Vol. 4, pp. 217–53.

Riggio, Milla Cozart (ed.) (1999). *Teaching Shakespeare Through Performance*. New York: Modern Language Association of America.

Rocklin, Edward. (2005). *Performance Approaches to Teaching Shakespeare*. Urbana: National Council of Teachers of English.

Svensson, Lennart. (1984). "Skill in Learning and Organizing Knowledge". *The Experience of Learning*. F. Marton, D. Hounsell, and N. Entwhistle (eds). Edinburgh: Scottish Academic Press.

Wolf, Hirst. (1981). *John Keats*. Boston: Twayne Publishers.

Chapter 1: Thinking Like Shakespeare
Books and Essays

Arikha, Noga. (2007). *Passions and Tempers: A History of the Humours*. New York: Harper Collins.

Bickerton, Derek. (2009). *Adam's Tongue: How Humans Made Language, How Language Made Humans*. New York City: Hill and Wang.

Brown, Colin M., and Hagoort, Peter. (eds). (2001). *The Neurocognition of Language*. Oxford, United Kingdom: Oxford UP.

Deacon, Terrence. (1997). *The Symbolic Species: The Co-evolution of Language and the Human Brain*. London: Penguin Books.

Hagoort, Peter, and Levelt, Willem. (2009). "The Speaking Brain." *Science*, Vol. 326, No. 5951, October 16, 2009.

Lovejoy, Arthur O. (1936). *The Great Chain of Being: A Study of the History of An Idea*. Cambridge: Harvard UP.

McDonald, Russ. (2001). *The Bedford Companion to Shakespeare: An Introduction with Documents*. Boston: Bedford/St. Martins.

Molfese, Dennis, and Segalowitz, Sidney. J. (eds). (1988). *Brain Lateralization in Children: Developmental Implications*. New York: Guildford Press.

Paster, Gail Kern. (2004). *Humouring the Body: Emotions and the Shakespearean Stage*. Chicago: University of Chicago Press.

Pinker, Steven. (1997). *How the Mind Works*. London: Penguin Books.

———. (1994). *The Language Instinct*. London: Penguin Books.

Rubenzer, Ronald. (1982). *Educating the Other Half: Implications of Left/Right Brain Research*. Reston: The Council for Exceptional Children.

Sahin, Ned, Pinker, Steven, Cash, Sydney S., Schomer, Donald, and Halgen, Eric. (2009). "Sequential Processing of Lexical, Grammatical, and Phonological Information Within Broca's Area." *Science*, Vol. 326, No. 5951, October 16, 2009.

Tillyard, E. K. (1961 reprint). *The Elizabethan World Picture: A Study of the Idea of Order in the Age of Shakespeare, Donne, and Milton*. New York: Vintage Books.

Wells, Stanley. (2003). *Shakespeare For All Time*. Oxford: Oxford UP.

Chapter 2: Stages of Green: *A Midsummer Night's Dream*
Books and Essays

Brook, Peter. (1968). *The Empty Space: A Book About the Theatre; Holy, Rough, Immediate*. New York: Simon and Schuster.

Gabriel, Egan. (2006). *Green Shakespeare: From Ecopolitics to Ecocriticism. Accents on Shakespeare.* New York: Routledge.

Frye, Northrup. (1995). *A Natural Perspective: The Development of Shakespearean Comedy and Romance.* 2nd edn. New York: Columbia UP.

———. (1986). *On Shakespeare.* New Haven: Yale UP.

Fuchs, Elinor, and Chaudhuri, Una. (eds). (2002). *Land/Scape/Theater.* Ann Arbor: University of Michigan Press.

Garrard, Gary. (2004). *Ecocriticism (The New Critical Idiom).* London: Routledge.

Latham, Minor White. (1930). *The Elizabethan Fairies: the Fairies of Folklore and the Fairies of Shakespeare.* New York: Columbia UP.

Maranca, Bonnie. (1996). *Ecologies of Theatre.* New York: Routledge.

Thirsk, Joan. (1959). *Tudor Enclosures.* London: Routledge.

Van Boven, L., and Gilovich, T. (2003). "To do or to have? That is the question." *Journal of Personality and Social Psychology,* Vol. 85, pp. 1193–202.

Williams, Gary Jay. (1997). *Our Moonlight Revels: A Midsummer Night's Dream in the Theatre.* Iowa City: University of Iowa Press.

Film

A Midsummer Night's Dream (1935). Directed by William Dieter and Max Reinhardt.

A Midsummer's Night's Dream (1999). Directed by Michael Hoffman.

Web Materials

Center for Sustainable Practice in the Arts: http://www.sustainablepractice/org/. Last accessed January 4, 2011.

Chapter 3: The Problem of Power: *Measure for Measure*
Books and Essays

Boal, Augusto. (1993). *Theatre of the Oppressed.* New York: TCG.

Callaghan, Dympna. (2001). *A Feminist Companion to Shakespeare.* Hoboken, NJ: Wiley-Blackwell.

Chedgzoy, Kate. (2001). *Shakespeare, Feminism, and Gender.* New York: Palgrave Macmillan.

Gay, Penny. (1994). *As She Likes It: Shakespeare's Unruly Women.* London: Routledge.

James I. (1603). *Basilikon Doron.* London: E. Allde and E. White.

Erickson, Peter. (1985). *Patriarchal Structures in Shakespeare's Drama.* Berkeley: University of California Press.

Greenblatt, Stephen. (1989). *Shakespearean Negotiations: The Circulation of Social Energy in Renaissance England.* Berkeley: University of California Press.

Maclean, Ian. (1980). *The Renaissance Notion of Women: A Study in the Fortunes of Scholasticism and Medical Science in European Intellectual Life.* Cambridge: Cambridge UP.

Rutter, Carol. (1989). *Clamorous Voices: Shakespeare's Women Today.* New York: Routledge, Chapman, and Hall.

Stone, Lawrence. (1967). *The Crisis of the Aristocracy, 1558–1641,* Oxford: Oxford UP.

———. (1977). *The Family, Sex, and Marriage in England, 1500–1800*. London: Weidenfeld & Nicolson. New York: Harper & Row.

Weatherford, John W. (2001). *Crime and Punishment in the England of Shakespeare and Milton, 1570–1640*. Jefferson, NC: MacFarland.

Film

Measure for Measure (1979). Directed by Desmond Davis.

Measure for Measure (1994). Directed by David Thacker.

Chapter 4: The Rhetoric of Hate: *Othello*
Books and Essays

Artaud, Antonin. (Mary C. Richard, trans.). (1994). *The Theatre and Its Double*. New York: Grove Press.

Bernard, J. (1995). "Theatricality and Textuality: The Example of *Othello*." *New Literary History*, Vol. 26, pp. 931–49.

Brecht, Bertolt. (John Willett, trans.). (1977). *Brecht on Theatre: The Development of an Aesthetic*. New York: Hill and Wang.

Ghazoul, Ferial J. (1998). "The Arabization of Othello." *Comparative Literature*, Vol. 50, No. 1, pp. 1–31.

Hadfield, Andrew. (1998). "Race in *Othello*: The 'History and Description of Africa' and the Black Legend." *Notes and Queries*, Vol. 45, pp. 336–38.

Harris, Bernard. (2000). "A Portrait of a Moor." *Shakespeare and Race*, pp. 23–36. Catherine Alexander and Stanley Wells (eds). Cambridge: Cambridge UP.

Korhonen, Anu. (2005). "Washing the Ethiopian White: Conceptualizing Black Skin in Renaissance England." *Black Africans in Renaissance Europe*, pp. 94–112. T. F. Earle (ed.) Cambridge UP.

Loomba, Ania. (1989). *Gender, Race, Renaissance Drama*. Manchester, England: Manchester University Press.

Nicholl, Charles. (2007). *The Lodger: Shakespeare, His Life on Silver Street*. London: Allen Lane.

Xiaojing, Zou. (1998). "Othello's Color in Shakespeare's Tragedy." *College Language Association Journal*, Vol. 45, pp. 335–48.

Film

Othello (1952). Directed by Orson Welles.

Othello (1956). Directed by Sergei Jutkevitsh.

O (2001). Directed by Tim Blake Nelson.

Chapter 5: Art, Science, Mysticism, and *The Tempest*
Books and Essays

Brown, Paul. (1985). "'This thing of darkness I acknowledge mine': The Tempest and the Discourse of Colonialism." *Political Shakespeare: New Essays in Cultural Materialism*, pp. 48–71. Jonathan Dollimore and Alan Sinfield (eds). Ithaca: Cornell UP.

Loomba, Ania, and Orkin, Martin. (eds). (1998). *Post-Colonial Shakespeares*. London: Routledge.

Mebane, John S. (1989). *Renaissance Magic and the Return of the Golden Age: The Occult Tradition and Marlowe, Jonson, and Shakespeare*. Lincoln: Univ of Nebraska UP.

Pink, Dan. (2005). *A Whole New Mind: Why Right Brainers Will Rule the Future*. New York: Penguin Books.

Levack, Brian (ed.). (2003). *The Witchcraft Sourcebook*. London: Routledge.

Loomba, Ania. (2002). *Shakespeare, Race, and Colonialism*. Oxford: Oxford UP.

Mowat, Barbara A. (2001). "Prospero's Book." *Shakespeare Quarterly*. Vol. 52, No. 1, pp. 1–33.

Scarre, Geoffrey. (1987). *Witchcraft and Magic in Sixteenth and Seventeenth Century*. Atlantic Highlands, NJ: Humanities Press International.

Vaughn, A. T., and Vaughn, Virginia M. (1991). *Shakespeare's Caliban: A Cultural History*. Cambridge: Cambridge UP.

Film

Forbidden Planet (1956). Directed by Fred M. Wilcox.

Prospero's Books (1991). Directed by Peter Greeneway.

The Tempest (1960). Directed by George Schaefer.

The Tempest (1982). Directed by Paul Mazursky.

The Tempest (2010). Directed by Julie Taymor.

Yellow Sky (1948). Directed by Richard Wellman.

Web Materials

Montaigne, Michel De. "Essays." Great Literature Online, 1997–2011: http://montaigne.classicauthors.net/Essays/Essays4.html. Last accessed January 4, 2011.

General Sources on Acting, Production, and Shakespeare Studies
Books and Essays

Barton, John. (1984). *Playing Shakespeare*. London: Methuen.

Berry, Cicely. (1992). *The Actor and the Text*. New York: Applause.

Berry, Ralph. (1990). *On Directing Shakespeare*. New York: Viking Press.

———. (1988). *Shakespeare and Social Class*. Atlantic Highland, NJ: Humanities Press International, Inc.

Bloom, Harold. (1999). *Shakespeare: The Invention of the Human*. London: Fourth Estate.

Dash, Irene. (1981). *Wooing, Wedding, and Power: Women in Shakespeare's Plays*. New York: Columbia UP.

Drakakis, John. (ed.) (1985). *Alternative Shakespeares*. New York: Methuen.

Dusinberre, Juliet. (1996). *Shakespeare and the Nature of Women*. 2nd edn. New York: St. Martin's.

Fraser, Antonia. (1984). *The Weaker Vessel*. New York: Knopf.

French, Marilyn. (1981). *Shakespeare's Division of Experience*. New York: Summit.

Hudson, A. K. (1963). *Shakespeare in the Classroom*. London: Heinemann.

Jardine, Lisa. (1989). *Still Harping on Daughters: Women and Drama in the Age of Shakespeare*. New York: Columbia UP.

Jorgens, Jack. (1991). *Shakespeare on Film*. University Press of America.

Kott, Jan. (1974). *Shakespeare Our Contemporary*. New York: Norton.

Linklater, Kristin. (1992). *Freeing Shakespeare's Voice*. New York: TCG.

Martineau, Jane, and Shawe-Taylor, Desmond. (eds). (2003). *Shakespeare in Art*. London: Merrill Publishers.

Packer, Tina, and Whitney, John O. (2000). *Power Plays: Shakespeare's Lessons in Leadership and Management*. New York: Simon and Schuester.

Rodenberg, Patsy. (2004). *Speaking Shakespeare*. New York: Palgrave Macmillan.

Shafer, Elizabeth. (2000). *Ms-Directing Shakespeare: Women Direct Shakespeare*. New York: Palgrave Macmillan.

Tucker, Patrick. (2002). *Secrets of Acting Shakespeare: The Original Approach*. New York: Routledge.

Van Tassel, Wesley. (2000). *Clues to Acting Shakespeare*. New York: Allworth Press.

Web Materials:

Complete Works of Shakespeare: http://shakespeare.mit.edu/works.html/. Last accessed January 4, 2011.

Folger Shakespeare Library: http://www.folger.edu/. Last accessed January 4, 2011.

Royal Shakespeare Company: http://www.rsc.org.uk/. Last accessed January 4, 2011.

Shakespeare and Company: http://www.shakespeare.org/. Last accessed January 4, 2011.

Shakespeare Birthplace Trust: http://www.shakespeare.org.uk/. Last accessed January 4, 2011.

Shakespeare Web: http://shakespeare.com/. Last accessed January 4, 2011.

Shakespeare in Quarto: http://www.bl.uk/treasures/shakespeare/homepage.html. Last accessed January 4, 2011.

Shakespeare's Globe: http://www.shakespeares-globe.org/. Last accessed January 4, 2011.

Shakespeare's World: http://shakespeare.emory.edu/. Last accessed January 4, 2011.

Glossary of Terms

Alienation effect: Bertolt Brecht's theory that audience empathy should be minimized in order to maintain intellectual objectivity. (See V-effect.)

Apron stage: A stage on which most of the playing space extends beyond the frame of the proscenium arch. In the Tudor/Stuart era, playhouses had apron stages that were surrounded by audience on three sides.

Back-story: The events and circumstances that existed before the action of the play begins. Actors often develop detailed back-stories to aid in the creation of fully realized characters.

Blank verse: Unrhymed verse used extensively in Elizabethan and Jacobean drama.

Blocking: Performers' movement on the stage, which is usually coordinated by the production's director.

Catharsis: According the Greek philosopher and dramatic theorist Aristotle, tragedy serves an important communal function by evoking catharsis, a release or purgation of excessive emotions, especially pity and fear.

Convention: A standardized dramatic feature that is usually nonrealistic, but accepted by the audience as part of the world of the play. Soliloquies and asides, in which the actor speaks directly to the audience, are examples of dramatic conventions.

Correspondence theory: An extension of the Renaissance doctrine of natural order, correspondence theory maintained that everything in the universe had analogies and correlations to other entities in the cosmos.

Doubling: The practice of casting a single actor in multiple roles.

Dramaturg: A literary and historical advisor on a theatrical production.

Empathy: The audience's sensation of emotional identification with a character.

Environmental Theatre: A form of theatre associated primarily with Richard Schechner of the Performance Group. Environmental theatre reimagines the performance space, using all elements of the "environment," and eliminating traditional separations between audience and performers.

Epic Theatre: A dramatic form, most closely associated with Bertolt Brecht and the Berliner Ensemble, which focuses on eliciting intellectual and rational responses to social issues, rather than evoking audience empathy.

Ethos: A type of rhetorical persuasion based on the credibility of the speaker and his/her ethical values.

Exposition: Revelation of important information that occurred before the beginning of the play. Exposition is usually, but not always, relayed early in the play through dialogue.

First Folio: A commemorative collection of Shakespeare's plays assembled by two of his fellow theatre company members and published in 1623, seven years after the playwright's death.

Foot prosody: Meter based on the number of beats per line and the type of metrical foot.

Found space: Performance space that is converted from another use, such as airplane hangers, bars, and warehouses.

Fourth wall: Theatrical convention that requires the audience to pretend that they are viewing a scene through an imaginary fourth wall.

Great Chain of Being: Also called the "scala naturae," or natural ladder, the Great Chain of Being represents a Renaissance conception of the hierarchical arrangement of everything in the universe.

Groundling: In the professional playhouses of Tudor/Stuart England, the groundlings occupied cheap standing places in front of the stage.

Humours: Renaissance medical theory that contended that the human body was governed by organic fluids called humours that influenced both physical health and personality.

Iambic pentameter: The most common form of meter in Shakespeare's plays, consisting of five pairs of unstressed syllables followed by stressed syllables.

Lab lit: Sub-category of the science fiction category that focuses on the realistic portrayal of scientists and scientific principles.

Logos: A form of rhetorical persuasion based on reasoning, accuracy, and facts.

Magic if: An acting exercise that poses the question, "How would I respond in this situation?"

Masque: A form of courtly entertainment characterized by lavish costumes and settings, dance, and actors portraying allegorical characters.

Method acting: Set of acting techniques, often associated with the Russian teacher Constantin Stanislavsky, that helps performers to personally identify with their character.

Mise en scene: The visual elements of a theatrical space, including scenery and movement.

Multifocus: A type of staging in which more than one action occurs simultaneously in different areas of the performance space.

Objective: A character's goal in a scene or play.

Obstacle: The obstacle stands in the way of a character achieving his/her goal (objective). The juxtaposition between objective and obstacle creates the conflict that is at the core of virtually all plays.

Onnagata: Male performers who impersonate female roles in Japanese Kabuki theatre.

Pathos: A rhetorical form that relies on emotion to persuade the listener.

Point of attack: In dramatic structure, the place in the story at which the plot commences.

Poor theatre: A reaction against "rich" entertainment forms, such as television and film, Poor theatre was invented by Polish director Jerzy Grotowski, who called for elimination of all nonessential theatrical elements, such as scenery and recorded sound.

Problem play: A dramatic text that defies traditional genre distinctions, and usually examines a pressing social question.

Scansion: Analysis of the structure and meter of a verse line.

Science play: Dramatic genre featuring the principles of math and science, and/or the work of scientists and mathematicians.

Scoring: The process of marking the stresses in a verse line.

Shareholders: A group of investors who shared financial and decision-making power in the Elizabethan theatre. Shakespeare was a shareholder in the Globe Theatre.

Soliloquy: A type of monologue that is spoken directly to the audience.

Sonnet (Shakespearean): Poem having 14 lines, with a rhyme pattern of ABAB CDCD EFEF GG.

Spectacle: Theatrical elements that engage the senses, such as scenic design, costume, sound, and special effects.

Tableaux vivant: "Living pictures" formed by actors and utilized in Augusto Boal's Theatre of the Oppressed.

Theatre of Cruelty: Antonin Artaud's radical form of theatre that utilized sensory overload to circumvent the audience's intellectual response and force confrontation of mankind's hidden cruelty.

Theatre of the Oppressed: Form of interactive theatre invented by Augusto Boal.

Unities: Neoclassical interpretation of Aristotle's tragic theory. Strict adherence to the "three unities" requires that dramatic action takes place in one day, one place, and concerns a single plot line.

V-effekt: German term, literally "verfremdungseffkt," invented by Bertolt Brecht to refer to the alienation effect.

Verisimilitude: "Likeness to truth," a defining goal of neoclassical, realist, and naturalist theatre. The concept of verisimilitude has its foundation in Aristotle's observation that theatre is an outgrowth of a natural human impulse to imitate.